Denali National Park & Preserve, Alaska

Backcountry Companion

by Jon Nierenberg

The Alaska Natural History Association is a non-profit organization whose mission is to enhance understanding and conservation of the natural, cultural and historical resources of Alaska's public lands through education, public information and research.

Proceeds from the sale of this book support the education and scientific programs at Denali National Park and Preserve.

Author and photographer: Jon Nierenberg
Designer: Donna Gates King
Cover photo: Roy Corral

Published by the Alaska Natural History Association,
750 West Second Avenue, Suite 100, Anchorage, Alaska 99501
Printed in Hong Kong by Global Interprint

www.alaskanha.org

CONTENTS

This book is dedicated to all the people, rangers and volunteers who have worked the backcountry desk at Denali's visitor center. Through their patience and dedication they have enabled the park to allow a quality wilderness experience for all backcountry users without compromising the goals of the wilderness ethic.

ACKNOWLEDGMENTS

Without the help of many people this book would not be possible, and I wish to acknowledge their assistance here. There are many people who helped in the technical preparation of this project. Bryan Swift and the staff of Denali National Park provided guidelines for the book's format. Donna Gates King worked her usual magic in transforming a straightforward text into a unique book, with her graphics and lay-out work. Judith Brogan and Frankie Barker with the Alaska Natural History Association edited and reviewed text from draft manuscript to finished book and enabled me to continue the project to the end. The use of the Swifts' word processor allowed me to finish the text before 1995, and my old typewriter appreciates this very much! Every hiker has a special partner, who always seems to be there when that hard peak is climbed, or that uncrossable river is crossed. Al Smith is my Denali partner, and without his assistance many of my best hikes would only be dreams. It always seems that authors are thanking their parents for one thing or another, and I'm no exception. While my parents have had little to do with the Denali backcountry, they did instill in me an appreciation for nature, and supported me in all my endeavors. Without them, my life would be very different. There is one special person who provided unflagging support and commitment, above and beyond what I could have hoped for. Three years ago I went to Kathy Loux, Denali's Alaska Natural History Association branch manager and good friend, with the idea for a backcountry book for Denali. Since then, she has been a strong driving force, pushing me on when I was ready to give up. More than anyone else, Kathy has earned the recognition she deserves. A special thanks to you, Kathy! A project such as this can only come about by a team effort, and to all of the team, I wish to express my grateful thanks.

INTRODUCTION

Congratulations! You and your backpack made it to Denali National Park. You want to hike for a week in the park's backcountry and need to know what to expect. After searching around, you find a park ranger who directs you to the Visitor Center for information about backcountry hiking.

After a short walk you find the Visitor Center and enter. You line up at the backcountry desk behind some other hikers. Finally it's your turn with the backcountry ranger. Your questions tumble out: "How much water should I carry? Where is the wildlife? Which area is most scenic? Why is the backcountry system so confusing? You're amazed to find the number of hikers in Alaska's best-known national park and that permits and bear-resistant food containers are required even for only an overnight hike? Most backcountry hikers in Denali National Park cover this same trail, and it is for you that I wrote this book. As I make my appointed rounds as a backcountry ranger for the National Park Service, I find myself answering the same questions over and over again. By reading this book you'll be a few steps ahead of the game and when you get your turn with the rangers at the backcountry desk, you'll be asking questions more specific to the trip you've already planned. Don't be overwhelmed by the system. Not only is Denali managed differently than most parks, you also will find few publications available to help prepare you for your journey. This book is the first to inform hikers about the terrain, some of the hazards, and other important information about the Denali Wilderness. Before stating what this book contains, it's necessary to know what it doesn't contain. This is not a trail guide, since with few exceptions (see pages 40, 59 and 73) no established trail system exists in the park backcountry. This book won't answer all your questions. It doesn't tell you where to hike, since that is your decision, but it can help you plan your trip. This book is designed to introduce backcountry visitors to what to expect at the park and can help answer your questions once you begin your hike. It discusses potential hazards of the backcountry, such as grizzly bear encounters, glacial river crossings, and trailless hiking, and describes details of different areas of the park.

Remember the title of this book—it is important. A backcountry "companion" is not a "guide." This book should not be your only source of information. Talk to backcountry rangers at the Visitor Center before beginning your trip. They can provide suggestions, site-specific descriptions, updates on conditions, and the necessary backcountry permit and bear-resistant food container.

Don't be overwhelmed by the preparations. You'll find the procedure worth the beauty that awaits those wishing to explore it. The park truly is a magical place.

HISTORY OF DENALI NATIONAL PARK AND PRESERVE

Congress initially established Denali National Park as Mount McKinley National Park in 1917, primarily to protect the unique wildlife found in its ecosystem. With some small additions in 1922 and 1932 the park boundary encompassed nearly two million acres. Final additions to the park came in 1980, when the Alaska National Interest Lands Conservation Act (ANILCA) became law. ANILCA established several new Alaska parks, such as Gates of the Arctic and Lake Clark, and increased the dimensions of Denali to nearly six million acres—about the size of Massachusetts. The park comprises three management areas—wilderness, new park, and preserve. The original boundaries of Mount McKinley National Park were designated in the new system as the Denali Wilderness. Except for the Park Road corridor and roadside campgrounds, this area is managed as a trailless wilderness with no fires or pets allowed. Most hikers entering the backcountry go into the Denali Wilderness. The 1980 additions to Denali are either part of new park additions or preserve. The primary difference between the two is management of wildlife. Preserve land allows sport hunting regulated under Alaska state game laws, and new park designation does not. Few hikers enter the new park lands, except mountaineers on the Mount McKinley massif and hikers in the Cantwell (southeast) area. Virtually no backpackers enter preserve areas. The vastness of the park is one of its most appealing features to hikers seeking a true "wilderness experience." Little has changed since the Athabascan hunters first made interior Alaska their home thousands of years ago. Park management relies on backcountry users to maintain the wilderness values for future generations.

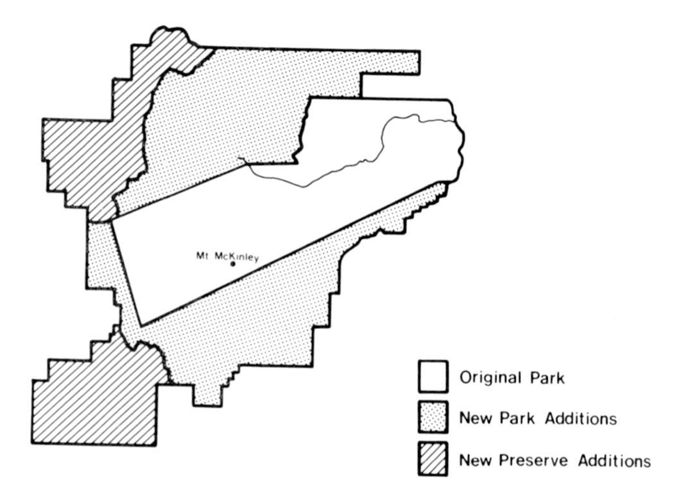

VEGETATION AND TERRAIN

Plants and the land they grow on are of utmost importance to the hiker—conditions and their effects on your mobility vary with location. Many are unfamiliar with tundra—the dominant ground-cover type in the park.

Wet tundra, the least desirable from the hikers' standpoint, can consist of open water, grass and willow hummocks, deep mud holes, and other unpleasant conditions. Hikers try to stay out of wet tundra areas, which usually occur in the lowest elevations. Moist tundra is generally passable though not the most comfortable to traverse. Footing is uneven on the spongy ground laced with hummocks and some water. Brush may be thick. Dry tundra, found at higher elevations, is by far the easiest terrain to hike over. Footing is more secure and brush is scattered to nonexistent.

Though dry tundra provides the best footing of the tundra types, hikers should take care not to rip up sections of the vegetative mat. Actually, hikers should consider all terrain to be fragile and parties should not walk in single file. If hikers spread out, impact is dispersed and lessened.

River bars are the main backcountry walkways for man and animals. Footing varies from secure to shaky on large, loose cobbles, but hiking a river bar is a preferred route of travel due to lack of thick vegetation, good visibility, low grade, and frequent landmarks for route finding. Most slopes in the backcountry, especially in the Alaska Range, are covered with scree and rotten rock. Scree is loose rock, usually found on unstable, steep slopes, lacking vegetation to hold the rock together. Walking on scree can be easy or terrifying, depending upon the slope, rock size, height, and what is below. Avoid crossing loose scree slopes above rivers. Sometimes the only way to get from one point to another is over scree, but don't attempt a dangerous crossing before assessing other options. Take time to evaluate your position and select the safest route possible. Scree walking is hard on knees and ankles, and you're more apt to make a mistake when you're tired and hurting. Don't depend on plants growing on scree slopes for support. They dislodge easily, and by using them as handholds you may endanger the plant's life—and your own.

Thorofare River

WILDLIFE

Although considered a prime area for viewing wildlife, the numbers and variety of wildlife in the park are lower than one might expect. The ecosystem of Denali National Park supports relatively few inhabitants due to the harsh climate. While a park like Yellowstone can sustain more animals per square mile (if human impact is not taken into account), the opportunity to observe wildlife is greater in Denali National Park. One reason is the lack of heavy, tall vegetation. Many of the major species prefer open tundra habitat. Hunting is illegal in the Denali Wilderness, and many of the animals have no fear of people. Whatever the reason, opportunities for observing the animal residents of the park abound.

Mammals found in the park include:

Shrew family—masked shrew, dusky shrew, arctic shrew, pygmy shrew.

Bat—little brown bat.

Pika family—collared pika.

Hare family—snowshoe hare.

Squirrel family—hoary marmot, arctic ground squirrel, red squirrel, northern flying squirrel.

Beaver family—beaver.

Muskrat, Vole, Lemming family—muskrat, northern red-backed vole, meadow vole, yellow-cheeked vole, tundra vole, hay mouse, northern bog lemming, brown lemming.

Porcupine family—porcupine.

Dog family—coyote, red fox, wolf.

Bear family—grizzly (brown) bear, black bear.

Weasel family—marten, short-tailed weasel, least weasel, mink, river otter, wolverine.

Cat family—lynx.
Deer family—moose, barren ground caribou.
Sheep family—Dall sheep.

The only amphibian in the park—the wood frog—is a member of the true Frog family. No other amphibians or reptiles live in the park.

Denali National Park is the summer home of many migratory birds, including eagles, falcons, waterfowl, finches, and warblers. The Alaska Natural History Association sales desk at the Visitor Center carries several bird identification books and a check list.

Red fox

WEATHER

Climate conditions at Denali National Park can vary considerably from day to day and even hour to hour. Weather changes are intensified due to the proximity of high peaks in the Alaska Range. Be prepared for anything—snow to 80°F. Though not common, snow does fall in summer months, especially near the range, and sunburn is a definite possibility, too. The rainfall column for the summer months may be misleading. Measurements make moisture levels seem low, but average weather for the summer months is cloudy skies and light rain.

	Average Temperature (-F°)		**Average Precipitation (inches)**	
Month	**Max.**	**Min.**	**Rain and/or**	**Snowfall**
January	10	-8	0.8	11
February	17	-4	0.6	10
March	25	1	0.5	9
April	39	15	0.5	6
May	54	29	0.9	Trace
June	65	39	2.3	Trace
July	66	42	2.8	Trace
August	63	39	2.5	Trace
September	52	30	1.6	4
October	33	14	1.0	13
November	18	1	0.8	15
December	8	-8	0.7	12
TOTAL			15.0	80

DENALI BACKCOUNTRY MANAGEMENT PLAN

Management of Denali National Park and Preserve differs from most other national parks in one major way—it does not have a trail system, either primitive or well developed. You won't find trail intersections with signs or markers, footbridges spanning creeks and rivers, or trail shelters because Denali has none of these.

The Denali Backcountry Management Plan emphasizes three main concepts—minimum impact, dispersion, and self-reliance—to retain the park's "wilderness feeling." Dispersion of hikers throughout the park dilutes negative effects on the environment and diminishes visual impact. It is unlikely that you will meet other parties once you leave the road corridor. Dispersion and minimum impact help preserve the flora and fauna.

Some find the idea of entering a wilderness with no trails or signs daunting. Many people wonder why the park doesn't develop a trail system. The Denali plan is an alternative to "developed" parks and is an excellent opportunity to see an unspoiled area without mobs of other hikers or constant reminders of civilization. Even inexperienced backpackers can enjoy the backcountry.

MINIMUM IMPACT

The concept of minimum impact is a simple one that most hikers have heard before: take nothing, disturb nothing, and leave nothing. Try to leave the wilderness as unspoiled as possible for those who follow to enjoy.

Carry out all your trash. Never bury garbage. This can destroy plant life, and the animals will probably dig it back up. Do not burn garbage. On-ground fires are not allowed in the Denali Wilderness. For human waste dig a small latrine hole about 5 to 6 inches deep, at least 300 feet (100 m) from any water source. Burn your toilet paper and cover the hole. Washing should also be done well away from water sources.

Try to avoid trampling the plants while hiking. If possible, walk on river bars. Spread out, and avoid walking in each other's footsteps when hiking in parties of two or more. Heavy hiking boots with hard lug soles tear up the tundra more than light-weight boots, and your choice of footwear should take this into account. Avoid leveling areas and moving rocks at campsites. Never pull up vegetation. Try to camp only one or two nights at the same site. Camp away from streams. Please pick up and carry out any trash you see anywhere.

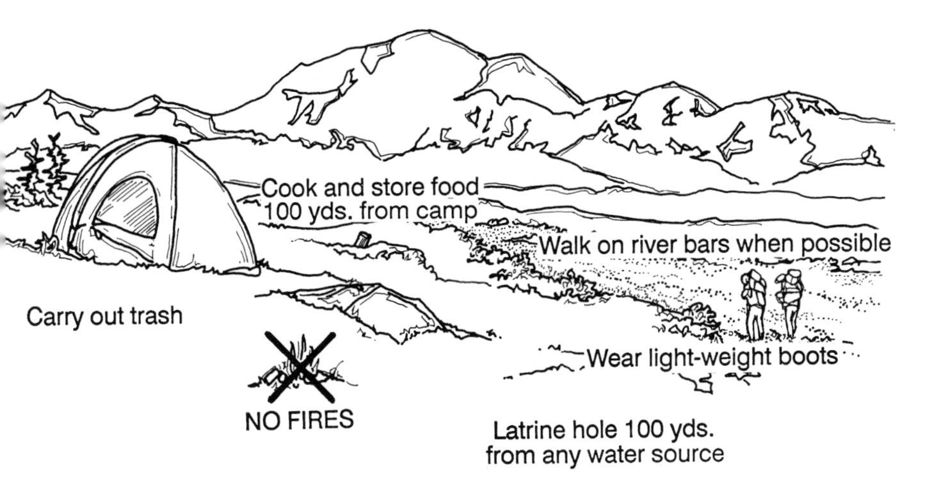

ORIENTATION AND ROUTE FINDING

Before entering Denali's backcountry, you should know how to read a topographic map and use a compass. You don't need to be an expert, but basic knowledge is an insurance policy against possible problems.

Although vast, the wilderness vistas of Denali are unobstructed by trees. Treeline is at about 2,500 feet (760 m), and most of the Denali Wilderness is above that. If you lose your bearings, climb to the nearest hill and consult your map. It's usually easy to find where you are (weather permitting). Remember, most rivers, except for the McKinley River, flow from south to north;

the mountain ranges are generally east to west; and the Park Road runs east to west between the Alaska and Outer Ranges.

Most hikers travel via river bars. With easy grades and unobstructed views, river bars are "good hiking" in Denali. There are few ridges to hike, and people accustomed to hiking in places like the White Mountains in New Hampshire are in for different hiking terrain. Avoid steep, scree-covered slopes as they can be unstable. Hiking cross country over wet tundra can demoralize an expedition. There are different types of tundra, and if you stumble into the wrong type, such as thick willows and poor footing, the going can get tough. It's safer to stay in the open where you can keep watch for bear and moose. Loose rock and scree cover many slopes, making footing uncertain and dangerous. Glaciers are a common feature of the Alaska Range. Take precautions when encountering these rivers of ice (see later chapter on glacier precautions). Glacial streams require caution when crossing, as their temperature, silt, and swiftness make them hazardous. Trips often must be modified because of undesirable conditions at planned river crossings (remember, no bridges!). Some hikers avoid crossings altogether by traveling up a river valley and back down it. Passes between river drainages in the ranges are few.

Whatever your choice of route, you should have and know how to read a map of the area. All U.S. Geological Survey (USGS) 1:63,360 and 1:250,000 scale topographic maps of the park are available for sale through the Alaska Natural History Association at the Visitor Center. Most have a contour interval of 100 feet, not 20 or 50 as many others do, which makes it more difficult to judge degree of slope. The park map 1:250,000 scale has contour intervals of 200 feet and is good for an overview, but it shouldn't replace the 15-minute (1:63,360) topographic maps. The backcountry ranger can help you select a map when you get your permit.

Inclement weather can obscure all landmarks, and this is when your compass will come in handy. Know how to use it. Remember to take into account magnetic declination, which is the error factor between true north and the magnetic north. Magnetic declination may vary from one map to another. If the weather deteriorates to the point that map and compass are not helpful, stay put and wait until later to hike on. You did remember that extra food, right?

BACKPACKER EQUIPMENT CHECKLIST

The gear listed below is only suggested. You may have experience with items not mentioned or have alternatives that have served you well. Just be sure your gear is appropriate for Alaska's backcountry, not the desert Southwest. Miscalculation can be humbling at best, disastrous at worst.

Clothing:

High-quality raingear (jacket/parka and pants/chaps). Ponchos are not recommended.
Jacket (wool, pile or other synthetic).
Cold-weather hat.
Mittens or heavy gloves.
Set of long underwear (synthetic or wool, no cotton).
Wool pants
Spare clothes (shirt, etc.).
Socks (wool or synthetic, warm-weather). Bring plenty of pairs.
Gaiters.
River-crossing footwear.
Hiking boots (every hiker has a preference. Be sure yours are recently waterproofed).
*Dress in layers and avoid cotton and down, as these fibers lose their insulating efficiency when wet. Casual synthetics should not be confused with synthetics designed specifically for outdoor use.

Sleeping Gear:

Sleeping bag (synthetic preferred over down). Should be rated to least 20° F.
Sleeping pad or air mattress (cutting tree boughs is illegal).
Tent (seam-sealed and waterproof). A tent is a must because of weather possibilities and insects, particularly mosquitoes. Tarps used as lean-tos are not practical.

Cooking Gear and Food:

Gas stove and fuel (no campfires are allowed in the Denali Wilderness).
Cooking utensils.

Food—Take plenty! Weather and hiking conditions mean you'll be burning more calories. Avoid foods known to attract bears, such as smoked and spiced food. All trash must be carried out, so minimize the canned goods and concentrate on dried alternatives. Selection of backpacking food in the park vicinity is limited.

Plastic bags (for trash and for keeping items dry).

Water bottles and water treatment items (such as filter).

Miscellaneous:

Orientation items (compass, maps).

First aid kit.

Waterproof matches.

Knife.

Signaling device (flare, whistle, flashlight).

Sunglasses.

Toilet articles.

Insect repellent (and/or headnet).

Camera with telephoto lens and film.

Water bottle and filter.

Binoculars.

WARNINGS AND HAZARDS

Before hiking in the Denali Wilderness, take the time to familiarize yourself with factors influencing the success and safety of your hike. If you're like most park visitors, primarily you are wondering about grizzly bears and the possible hazards they pose, but there are others. This chapter doesn't begin to cover them all completely, so be alert and wary. Bears:

Hikers can expect to find bears, either grizzly or black, anywhere in the park. Though bears are more often encountered in the back-country, they also occasionally wander into developed areas, such as around the hotel and campgrounds.

Bears in Denali are not tame or friendly. At best they tolerate people. Most avoid confrontations with humans, but should always be considered potentially dangerous. Don't approach them for any reason.

While in the park it is good to remember that you are in the bears' habitat, and things you do may affect one or many bears. Bears learn bad habits fast, and just one incident of a bear getting into a backpacker's food cache may result in a problem bear that associates hikers and food. Not only is this hazardous to other hikers, but it endangers the life of the bear itself. Be responsible for yourself, other hikers, and the bears and take precautions. To avoid a bear incident, try to avoid bears. Surprising a bear is no fun. Make noise when travelling in areas of low visibility, such as along winding streambeds and through thick vegetation. This gives the bear a chance to hear you and move off. Look for bear signs (prints, scat, diggings), and expect them anywhere in the park.

Most bear problems develop because of improper food storage and disposal practices. Most areas have no trees to hang food in (treeline in Denali is about 2,500 feet (760 m)) and food must be left on the ground. By following the guidelines listed below, you will reduce the chance that your food will attract a bear.

1. Pick your campsite carefully—Stay off game trails and away from streams or where you see fresh bear signs. Camp in an area of high visibility.
2. Keep your camp clean—Keep food odors away from your tent. Cooking should be done at least 100 yards (97 meters) away. Watch out for bears while cooking (kitchen should be in a high visibility area), and be ready to pack your food into a bear-

resistant container fast if you spot a bear. A bear resistant food container is required for any overnight stay in most areas of the park. You will get a container with your backcountry permit. They have proved very effective in thwarting bear problems. Keep the container nearby so food can quickly be stashed. Carry out all of your trash, and wash your cooking items. Store your food in the container at least 100 yards (97 meters) from the kitchen and the campsite.

3. Keep yourself free of cosmetic and food odors—Avoid use of any items such as perfumes or aftershaves, basically any cosmetic odor. Keep food items out of contact with your clothes.

   Don't sleep in clothes you've cooked in. While cooking wipe hands on a specific towel or bandanna that you store with the food. Remember, bears' sense of smell is their most highly developed.

Prevent bear problems by using bear resistant food containers.

Most backcountry hikers usually see bear from a distance. If you encounter a bear closeup, keep your wits about you and follow the proper procedure. Though advice listed below has been developed from experience, remember that bears are individuals, like people. Some are mellow, others nervous or skittish. Staying alert and taking precautions are your best insurance.

—**Distant bear unaware of your presence**—If the bear is a few hundred meters or more away and doesn't notice you, quietly move away. This is a "typical" bear. Alter your course if the bear is traveling towards you. Watch the bear as you move away.

—**Distant bear, aware and approaching**—Whatever you do, DON'T RUN! Running triggers a chase instinct in a bear, and it may charge you. Stay calm, gather all the members in your party together, stand where you are, wave your hands over your heads, keep your packs on, and speak loudly to the bear in a low voice. Usually the bear will move off.

—**Close bear, aware**—Observe the bear first. If it is uninterested in you, slowly move away. If the bear is interested in you and approaches, follow the steps in previous instructions.

—**Charging bear**—Bears rarely charge humans, and when it happens, usually it is a "false" or "bluff charge," intended to challenge or frighten you. Stay in control. Do not run (bears can run up to 40 miles per hour). Most charges are only a few

DO NOT RUN!

steps to a short run. Refer to steps in #2. If the bear continues to approach after you have tried the above instructions and contact seems certain, fall to your knees, bend over, put your head to the ground, and protect your head and neck with your arms and hands. Your pack should still be on as it protects your back. Lie still and quiet. Play dead. Wait for the bear to move away.

Although this section may unnerve some people, is is not meant to scare you out of the backcountry. As of 1996, Denali National Park has not had one death due to bear attack, and very few maulings. A good basic education on bear protocol, coupled with respect for the animals, has helped past backcountry users enjoy a safe stay, but it's up to us. Only responsible hikers ensure that this will continue.

Drinking water:

Giardia Lambdia occurs in rivers and streams throughout the park. These parasites can cause a severe reaction in humans known as beaver fever. Symptoms include nausea, diarrhea, cramps, and general misery. Play it safe and treat water for this and other contaminants before drinking. This means either using a filter specifically designed to remove small protozoan parasites, such as Giardia, or boiling the water. Since Giardia cysts are somewhat heat and cold resistant, boil the water for at least several minutes.

Choose your water source carefully. The safest are cold glacial streams taken near the headwaters, where the water flows quickly and has the least chance of already being contaminated. Still water, such as in tundra ponds, is a poor source due to concentration of contamination by beavers and other animals, even hikers.

Hypothermia:

Hypothermia is a cooling of the body core, but it is not just uncomfortable, it is disorienting and can be fatal. The cool, wet, windy weather common in Denali most of the summer combined with possible snowstorms, glacial river crossings, and strenuous terrain increase the danger.

The most important thing is to recognize the typical environments conducive to hypothermia and its beginning signs. Be sure you have proper gear and spare dry clothing. If you get wet and cold, stop to dry and drink hot liquids (one reason why a small backpacking stove is essential). Symptoms of hypothermia are dulled judgment, stiff hands and fingers, shivering, stumbling, slurred speech, drowsiness, and exhaustion. One deadly characteristic of hypothermia is not realizing when you have it, so it is important that members of your party observe each other for symptoms.

Treatment for hypothermia is simple—get dry and warm. Drink hot liquids. Do not drink alcoholic beverages! In advanced stages, the body is unable to rewarm itself, so a supplemental heat source, such as another body, is the best treatment. The key to beating hypothermia is prevention. Do not allow yourself to get beyond the mildly uncomfortable stage.

Critical Wildlife Habitat Closures:

Some areas in the park are closed to all travel, day-hiking, and backpacking. These Critical Wildlife Habitat Closures have been established to cover a number of different situations. For example, Sable Pass Closure is restricted because of high grizzly bear concentration. Other areas may be closed for reasons ranging from a recent bear incident, special denning or nesting areas, or unsafe wildlife conditions. Many of these closures vary from year to year so do not appear in the area descriptions found later in this book. Consult the ranger at the backcountry desk in the Visitor Center for updated information and detailed descriptions of closures. While some of the closures are posted, many are not, and it is your responsibility to know where the closures are and to stay out of them. Although some closures are established to protect the wildlife, many are meant to protect the park visitor, so view all closure areas as possible hazards.

Mining areas:

Denali and other Alaska national parks are different from most in the Lower 48 as mining is still permitted within 1980 addition boundaries. Most mining in Denali, active and defunct, is found in the Kantishna Mining District north of Wonder Lake. The majority are placer gold mines.

When hiking in Kantishna stay well away from the mining claims. Many claims are patented land, similar to private property; many include mining equipment and cabins, and all are privately owned. Do not enter a claim unless invited by the owner or operator. Maps and specific advice about Kantishna and the other areas of claims are obtained at the backcountry desk.

Glaciers and Mountaineering:

Denali National Park's numerous glaciers and peaks offer spectacular opportunities for mountaineers. Know your limitations. All glacier traversers should be familiar with glacial travel and crevasse rescue and have the necessary equipment (ropes, ice-axe, crampons, etc.). Most peaks higher than 7,000 feet (2134 meters) are covered year-round with ice and snow and are not casual climbs. Ask a park ranger about the skill required for a particular trip and to help determine the capabilities of your hiking party. This book's area descriptions, in the "Glaciers and Mountaineering" section, are basic comments and are not intended to be detailed enough to replace discussion with a ranger.

River Crossings:

River crossings in Denali's wilderness present special challenges even to experienced hikers because of near-freezing water temperatures. This section suggests proven safe methods of "reaching the other side."

Most streams in the park flow from glaciers and are cold, silty, and swift. Cold temperatures make leg cramps a hazard, silt makes determining river depth and other characteristics difficult, and swift currents have toppled many a hiker. Care can significantly reduce these dangers.

Cold water—Wear footgear that will keep your feet warm and also protect them from the rocky, uneven bottom. Most hikers use tennis shoes with wool or neoprene socks. Wear rainpants. You will still get wet, but they reduce the constant flow of icy water against your skin.

Crossing Thorofare River

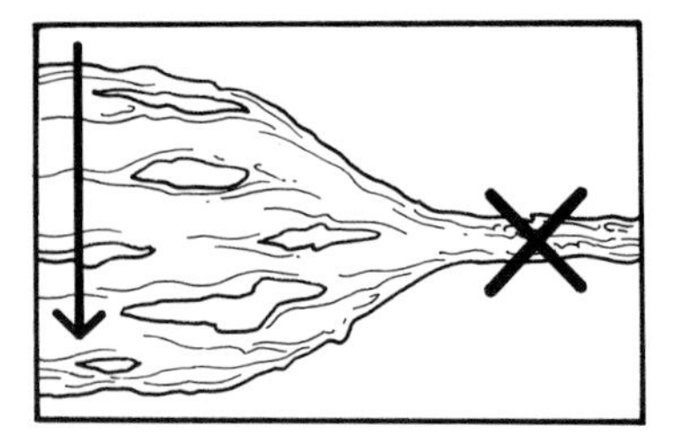

Silt—To determine channel depth, look at wave patterns. Differentiating between rock and standing waves helps. Throw a heavy rock into the water and listen for it to hit bottom. (Imagine all stream bottoms to be uneven.)

Swiftness—Crossing techniques will be detailed later, but I'll give you a few tips. Never cross in a straight line, but angle downstream so you are not fighting the current as much. Cross carefully but steadily. The longer you stay in, the more tired and cold you become. Shuffle your feet along the stream bottom, so you don't get spun around by the current. Do NOT look down as you cross, since the fast-moving dark water may make you dizzy (vertigo).

Proper preparation is important to a successful crossing. First, put all clothes and sleeping bags, along with other important gear, in waterproof bags. Have all things on your pack tied securely. Scout your route carefully. This may be the most important thing you can do to avoid a disaster. Though it is tempting to cross where the river is in one narrow channel, it is best to cross where the river is the widest and most braided. That is where the river runs slowest and shallowest. On a large river bar, such as on the McKinley River, you may need to backtrack to find good channels. Patience is the best guide.

Before "taking the plunge," unfasten your waist belt, and loosen the shoulder straps to your pack. If you fall in, your pack will float due to trapped airspace. If you are secured to your pack, you may find yourself face down in the river with your pack floating above you. Loosened straps allow you to quickly remove your pack. As you cross, don't hesitate to back out if you feel you can't make the crossing. With most rivers, if the water level is above knee-deep, it is a difficult crossing. If the level reaches above thigh-high, rethink trying your crossing elsewhere. Taller hikers have a distinct advantage. Rest between channels if tired and chilled.

Much about river crossing is acquired knowledge—and the more you do it, the better you become. By following the guidelines above, you have a good chance of successful crossings. Remember that these streams and rivers flow from glaciers, so the level varies from morning to night. During the warmest time of day, and directly after it, the level is high. For rivers such as the McKinley, try for an early crossing.

Below are some different techniques for river crossings:

Single-person crossing:

1. Stick (tripod) method—Enter the channel facing upstream, using a stick (approximately the height of the individual) for balance. The stick held upstream and your legs comprise a tripod for stability. Slowly shuffle across the channel. Don't raise the stick far off the stream bottom, or it may be swept away. A less stable variation of this method is to cross perpendicular to the stream flow.
2. Sideways method—By crossing sideways to the current flow, resistance to the current is reduced. With no stick for support, you must move more with the current and often end up far downstream from the starting point. The emphasis here is not on secure footing along the streambed, but rather on constantly moving with the current towards the other side. You may be able to cross more quickly than with the stick method.

Two-person crossing:

1. Modified stick method—One person, usually the strongest of the pair, follows the technique described in the single-person technique. The second person is directly behind the first, holding onto that person's waist. This way, the first person breaks the current flow, while the second person steadies the first. Remember to stay in line.
2. Arm link method—As in the solo sideways method, you cross perpendicular to the current. Link elbows, hold your arms close to your bodies, and cross. The upstream person breaks water for the downstream person. Stay in line.

Sideways method

Small-group crossing:

1. Modified stick method—Same as above, but many people behind the leader.
2. Shoulder grasp method—Face each other in a small circle, and grasp arms just below the armpits. Slowly enter the current. As you enter an area of faster current, the group will slowly be spun around. Don't fight all of the spinning tendency. Slowly move downstream and across.
3. Pole method—From personal experience, this is by far the best method for crossing in groups of three or more. Similar to the arm link, but use a long, straight pole to grasp under the linking arms. The pole adds stability and ensures the members stay in line. Use this technique only if you can find a driftwood pole, as cutting wood is prohibited.

Rope methods have not been mentioned because, if used incorrectly, they threaten drowning. DO NOT use a rope unless you have experience with this method. Never tie yourself onto a rope while crossing.

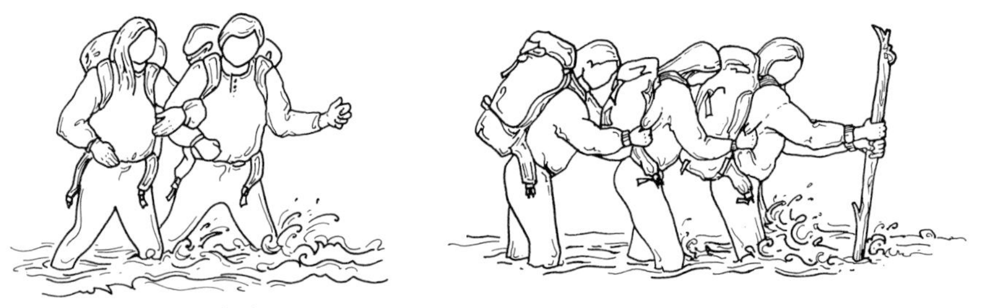

Arm link method *Pole method*

In summary, all glacial stream crossings should be taken seriously. Preplan carefully. Spend time to prepare yourself and your gear. Scout the river in detail. Be prepared for possible problems. Know your limits, and don't hesitate to back off and try again (or another day). Be aware of hypothermia. By following this advice, you will be able to cross these glacial streams and enter territory previously inaccessible to you.

—BACKCOUNTRY REGULATIONS

Regulations pertaining to backcountry use vary in different areas of the park. The park is divided into three parts: Denali Wilderness, Denali National Park Additions, and Denali National Preserve. Most hikers will only visit the backcountry in the Denali Wilderness, but a few will enter the Additions when hiking in the Kantishna Hills and near Cantwell. Listed below is a summary of basic, but not all-inclusive, regulations pertaining to the entire park.

	Denali Wilderness	**Denali NP Additions**	**Denali Preserve**
Campfires/groundfires	NO	YES	YES
Firewood source	no fires	—Dead and Down—	
Firearms	NO	YES	YES
Pets	NO	—Not recommended—	
Aircraft access	YES	YES	YES
Snowmachine access	NO	YES	YES
Sport fishing	YES	—With state license—	
Sport hunting	NO	NO	YES
Subsistence Hunting/Fishing	NO	—As authorized—	
Bear resistant food Containers Required	YES (some units)	NO	NO
Campsites .5 miles or more from Park Road AND out of sight of all roads.	YES	YES	YES
Backcountry unit quota System apply	YES	NO	NO
BACKCOUNTRY PERMIT REQUIRED	YES	YES	YES

BACKCOUNTRY PERMIT PROCEDURE

Backcountry permits are issued free to all wishing to hike in Denali National Park and Preserve on an overnight trip or longer. Day hikers are not required to have a permit but should still stop by the backcountry desk at the Visitor Center for information about their hike.

The first step in obtaining a backcountry permit is trip selection. With no trails, this process can present problems to the novice. This book provides basic information about what is physically out in the park and what to expect. Trip selection depends on how much time you have, your abilities, type of gear, and specific interests of the group (glaciers, canyons, etc.). Weather conditions, availability of transportation into the park, and numbers of hikers already in popular units can change your original plans. Be flexible.

Once you know where you want to go, even only generally, go to the backcountry desk and talk with a park ranger. This will help define your trip further and you can obtain a permit. By signing a backcountry permit, the individual or group concurs that rules and regulations are understood and will be followed.

In accordance with the Backcountry Management Plan, specific units are assigned for specific nights. Some units are quite large with many camping areas. Your party must be in the assigned unit for each specific night to avoid overloading another unit. If plans change and you cannot stay in the unit assigned, you should exit the backcountry and contact a ranger for assistance.

The backcountry permit must always be in plain view, attached to your backpack or tent. When you return from your trip, you must return it to the backcountry desk. The returned permit is an important record of your travel plans should anyone contact the Park Service to locate you. The Park Service does not automatically launch a search if a party is late. Leave a copy of your plans with a friend or relative, so if you have not returned on time, they can alert the park to check up on you.

Most backcountry units along the Park Road and in the Denali Wilderness require the use of a bear-resistant food container (BRFC) for overnight stays. These black plastic cylinders deter food-related bear incidents. The ranger at the backcountry desk will explain how to use them. The program has proved effective and soon will be adopted at other parks with high bear populations.

If one is assigned, failure to use the BRFC in certain units is a violation of your backcountry permit. Even where the containers are not required, I recommend their use. They are free (at the time of this printing) and can be conveniently obtained when you get your permit. If your group is large, you may need more than one. Another will be issued. Return containers promptly after your hike, to ensure enough for other hikers.

Once you get a permit and a BRFC, you'll want to check out transportation into the park. During most of the season private vehicle traffic into the park is restricted. Most backpackers use the shuttle bus system. The Visitor Center provides schedules and other information about the buses. Hikers can get off almost anywhere along the Park Road, so be sure you know where the best starting point is for your trip. Again, the park ranger at the backcountry desk can help you.

Check your pack before boarding the bus. Make sure you have all items needed for the trip. Remember, there are no services in the park west of the hotel area.

USE OF AREA DESCRIPTIONS——

A few explanations are necessary before you use the following area descriptions to help plan your trip into the backcountry. Each area is an arbitrary unit, usually divided from other areas by obvious natural features. The first part of an area description lays out the boundaries of the area to be discussed and explains what is found there.

The section titled "Flora and Terrain" does not list the types of flowers and rocks found there, it tells what type of walking you can expect, given plant, soil, and topography. Hazardous hiking conditions and vegetation types as they affect footing are also discussed from the hiker's perspective.

The "Wildlife" section describes fauna of the park and type of habitat where it is most commonly found. Don't expect to find specific nesting or calving sites. Remember, bears are everywhere, and take proper precautions.

The "Rivers and Streams" section notes possible hazardous crossings but is obviously not exhaustive. Flow and speed in all rivers and streams in the park can vary dramaticaliy with glacier melt and rainfall, so be prepared. I do not recommend specific sites for crossing rivers because of the constantly changing currents and channels of glacial rivers.

"Glaciers and Mountaineering" mentions most glaciers and mountain climbs of any note. Many times, such as in the Outer Range areas, there are no glaciers or true mountaineering peaks, and this section may be used to note nontechnical mountains to ascend. Many times this section will not include all peaks that afford a good view. I leave it up to you to find more to climb.

Many area descriptions end with a "Special Note" section to cover anything from noting an established trail to specific hazards from mining. Pay particular attention to these sections!

Remember, these areas are large, varied, and described in general terms with little detail.

BACKCOUNTRY AREA DESCRIPTIONS

I have divided the Denali backcountry into five sections for convenience of description—the Alaska Range, Outer Range, Kantishna Hills, Park Additions, and Mount McKinley and other peaks. The Alaska Range describes the area to the north and south of the Alaska Range from the eastern park boundary to the west boundary of the Denali Wilderness. The Outer Range details the long mountain chain north of and parallel to the Alaska Range from Nenana River to Toklat River. The Kantishna Hills section describes the area west of the Outer Range to the north and west end of the hills. The Park Additions cover the lands added to the park with the 1980 ANILCA legislation (except for the Kantishna Hills) and Denali National Preserve. Finally, the section on mountaineering briefly describes the Mount McKinley mountain massif and associated peaks.

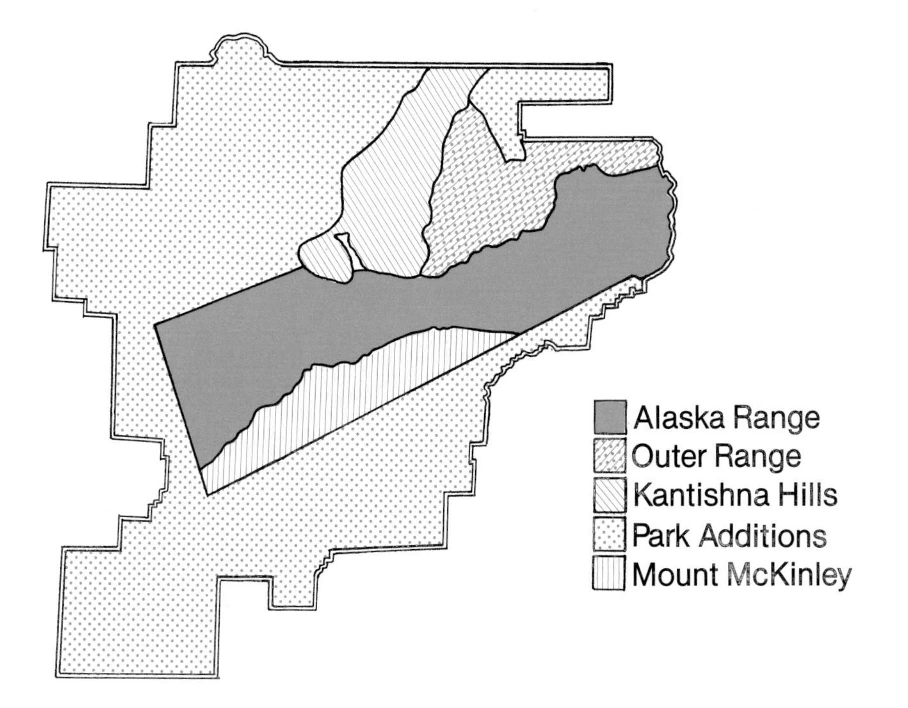

ALASKA RANGE

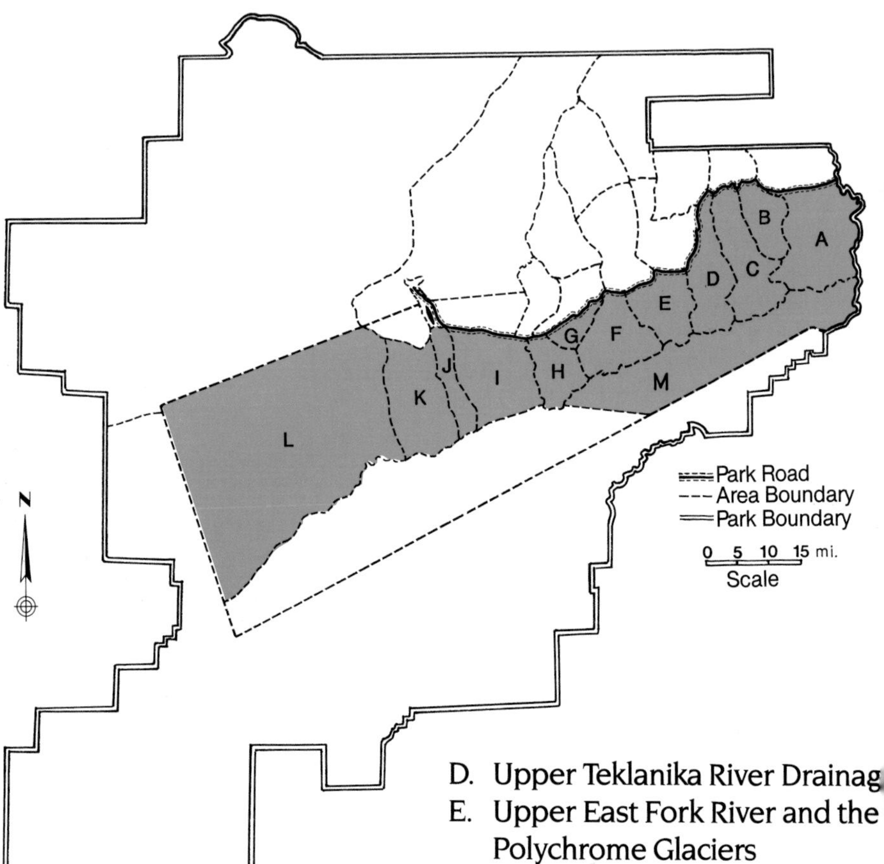

A. Riley Creek, Jenny Creek and the Triple Lakes
B. Upper Savage River Drainage
C. Upper Sanctuary River Drainage
D. Upper Teklanika River Drainag
E. Upper East Fork River and the Polychrome Glaciers
F. Upper Toklat River Valleys
G. Highway and Thorofare Passes
H. Mount Eielson and Upper Thorofare River
I. Upper McKinley Bar and Pirat Creek Drainage
J. McGonagall Pass
K. Muddy River Drainage
L. The West End
M. The South Side

Riley Creek Jenny Creek, and the Triple Lakes

This area in the eastern end of the park encompasses two main drainages. Riley Creek flows east and north from the eastern slopes of Fang Mountain, past the entrance of the Park Road to the Nenana River. Along the way, many side streams enter Riley Creek. Between the Riley Creek drainage and the eastern park boundary is the small valley where the Triple Lakes are found. Jenny Creek begins in the hills to the north of Riley Creek and flows in a western direction, meeting the Savage River near the Savage River Campground. Between these drainages rise gentle hills and ridges reaching the 5,000 feet (1,500 m) mark. Old glacial remains appear in the vicinity of upper Riley Creek.

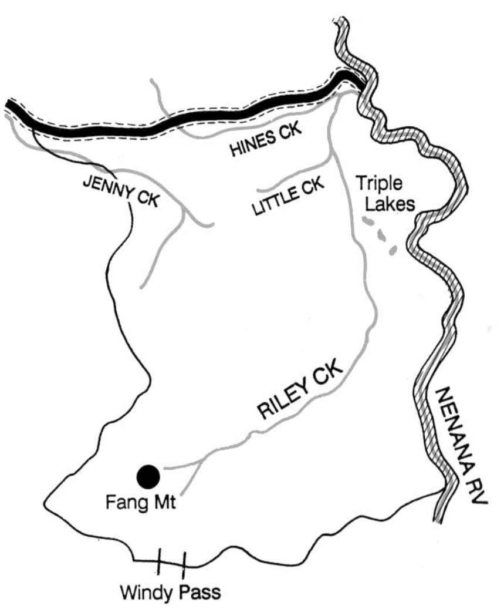

Flora and Terrain:

Vegetation varies from some dry tundra found only in the highest elevations to thick taiga spruce forests. Most of the area sustains a minimum of low brush cover, so cross-country travel is difficult. Spruce forest is very well developed near Triple Lakes. There are no glacial river bars in this area, but many sections of Riley Creek and other streams flow over a small gravel bar, making travel easier.

Wildlife:

Dall sheep occasionally are seen in the hills above Little Creek, and moose abound. Some grizzly and black bear occur here also. Grayling are found in the Triple Lakes.

Rivers and Streams:

Riley Creek is the major large waterbody that may pose a crossing problem. Since it doesn't flow over a wide gravel bar, it may be difficult to find a place where it braids into many shallow channels.

Glaciers and Mountaineering:

There are no true glaciers or mountaineering challenges in this area. Fang Mountain at 6,736 feet (2,053 m) is a difficult peak to climb, mainly because it is made up of very rotten rock and is a hazard to scramble over, although it is an impressive peak from its base.

Access from Park Road:

Mile 0 to Mile 12 or access from Parks Highway (Route 3):

The trail to Triple Lakes is 1/2 mile north of McKinley Village. The trailhead, on the western side of the highway, is usually marked with a small sign. Park vehicles well off the highway. A backcountry permit is required for overnight use.

Topographic maps:

Healy C-4, Healy C-5.

Ridge above Riley Creek

Upper Savage River Drainage

The Savage River flows north from the hills around Fang Mountain, past the Savage River Campground and the Park Road, into the Outer Range. Jenny Creek and Caribou Creek are the only tributaries of note. For its first 4 miles (6.5 km), the Savage River flows mostly over a small gravel bar in a valley with hills over 5,000 feet (1,500 m) on either side. For the 4 miles (6.5 km) to Jenny Creek and the 3 miles (4.9 km) to the road, the river is in the open tundra flats usually on a river bar. Except for Fang Mountain, the hills are rounded, gentle-sloped, and vegetated.

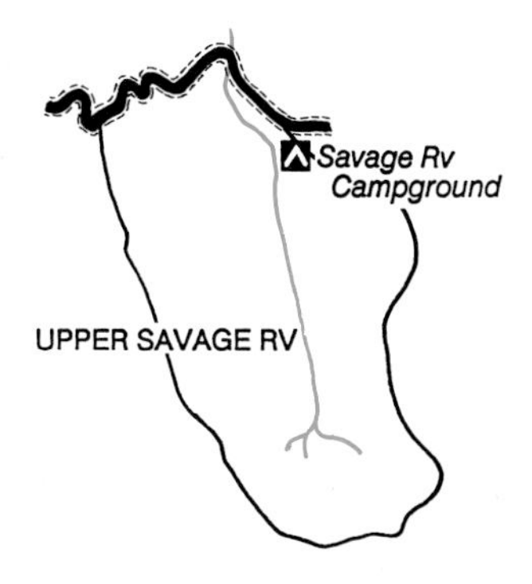

Vegetation and Terrain:

All types of tundra are found here—dry tundra on the highest elevations and moist tundra with some wet tundra bogs on the lower elevations, especially on the flats. Except in the high hills and on the watercourses, dwarf birch and dwarf willow are prominent.

Wildlife:

Moose are found throughout this area, grizzlies are sometimes seen, and caribou may be here early in the season. Beaver live along the upper Savage River and some of the side streams. Dall sheep use the hills year round. Grayling are found in Caribou Creek.

Rivers and Streams:

The Savage River is the only large river, and it usually poses no crossing difficulty with levels from ankle- to knee-deep.

Hikers on ridge above Savage River

Glaciers and Mountaineering:
There are no glaciers here. Fang Mountain has been previously discussed.

Access from Park Road:
Mile 12 to Mile 15 or access also from Savage River Campground.

Topographic Maps:
Healy C-5

Upper Sanctuary River Drainage

The Sanctuary River begins in the 6,000-foot (1,800-m) and higher peaks of the Alaska Range and flows due north for approximately 18 miles to the Sanctuary River Campground and the Park Road. The river's headwaters comprise three branches flowing from the range. The westernmost branch flows from the glaciers in Refuge Valley. The easternmost branch flows from Windy Pass. After the branches meet, the Sanctuary flows for 10 miles through a wide river valley, past hills reaching more than 5,500 feet (1,675 m), including the 5,899 feet (1,798 m) Double Mountain. The next 5 miles the river flows across the tundra flats to the Park Road

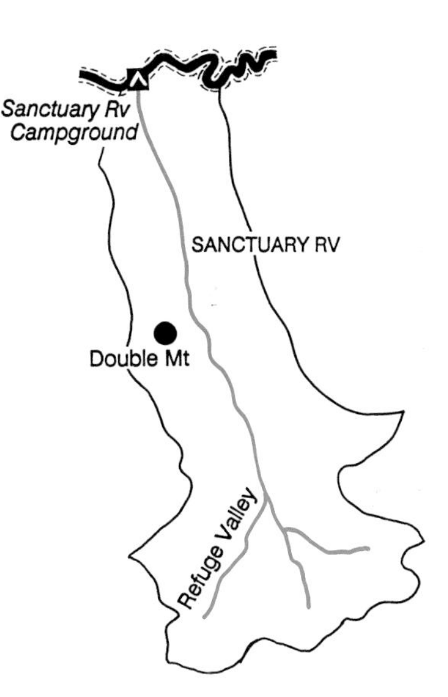

Vegetation and Terrain:

Exposed rock and scree slopes cover the sides of Refuge Valley and the north slopes of the Alaska Range. Vegetation here is usually dry tundra, similar to conditions in higher elevations downstream. As it passes through the valley, the vegetation along the Sanctuary River is dry tundra and willow. The tundra flats are moist and wet, supporting birch and willow. Some spruce grow along the river near the campground. Most of the Sanctuary River flows over a wide bar.

Wildlife:

Moose and grizzly bear are found in this area, as are caribou during the spring and summer months of the year, especially in Refuge Valley. Near the Alaska Range, small mammals such as marmot live in the rocks. Dall sheep are found on the slopes.

Rivers and Streams:

The Sanctuary River can be difficult to cross at times, but you usually can find a section where it braids. This is the only large river.

Glaciers and Mountaineering:

Small glaciers are tucked away on the north side of the Alaska Range, many in Refuge Valley. Double Mountain and other similar hills rise along the upper river. Their crumbly rock cover can make for hazardous climbing.

Access from Park Road:

Mile 22 to Mile 23 or access also from Sanctuary River Campground.

Topographic Maps:

Healy C-5, Healy B-5.

Upper Teklanika River Drainage

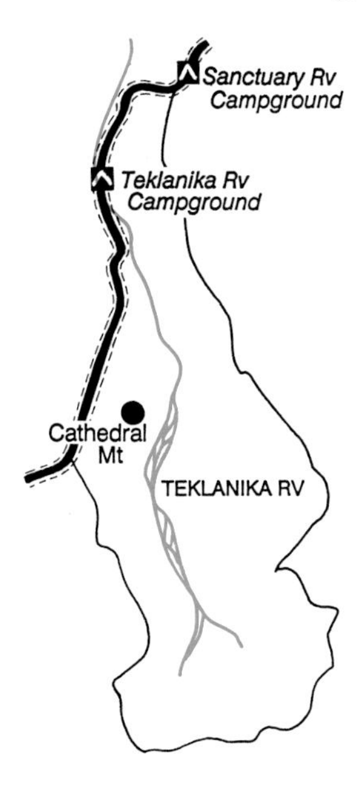

Two branches make up the headwaters of the Teklanika River, beginning at glaciers on the north side of the Alaska Range. After the branches meet the river flows over a wide gravel bar through a glacial valley for approximately 10 miles (17 km). Near the end of the relatively narrow valley the river flows past Cathedral Mountain (4,905 feet, 1,495 m) to the west and the junction of Calico Creek, a major feeder stream to the east. Calico Creek flows through a deep valley for about 5 miles, ending at Calico Pass which leads into the upper Sanctuary River. Past Cathedral Mountain, the Teklanika River flows through a much wider river valley another 3 miles (4.9 km) to the Park Road and then 7 miles (12 km) to the Outer Range.

Vegetation and Terrain:

Many slopes in the headwaters are scree and exposed rock with some dry tundra. Farther along the river the sides of the bar are lined with high willow and some alder. Once past Cathedral Mountain, spruce occasionally line the river, and heavy spruce forests line the river bar past the Teklanika River Bridge. Expect wet tundra and thick brush at lower elevations of the river.

Wildlife:

Sheep are commonly found on Cathedral Mountain as well as in the hills at the headwaters. Caribou may travel the bar and often use some of the passes near the glaciers to travel over to the Sanctuary River. Grizzly bears are common and moose are often seen along the flats north of Cathedral Mountain.

Rivers and Streams:

The Teklanika River is the only river hazard and can be deep at times. The large river bar enables hikers to find good crossings. Calico and Igloo creeks are easily traversed.

Glaciers and Mountaineering:

A few small glaciers, including the Cantwell, occur at the headwaters. No high peaks, but some challenging small ones (e.g., Cathedral and Double mountains) occur. Most are faced with exposed rock.

Access from Park Road:

Mile 25 to Mile 38.

Topographic Maps:

Healy B-5, Healy B-6, Healy C-5, Healy C-6.

ALASKA RANGE

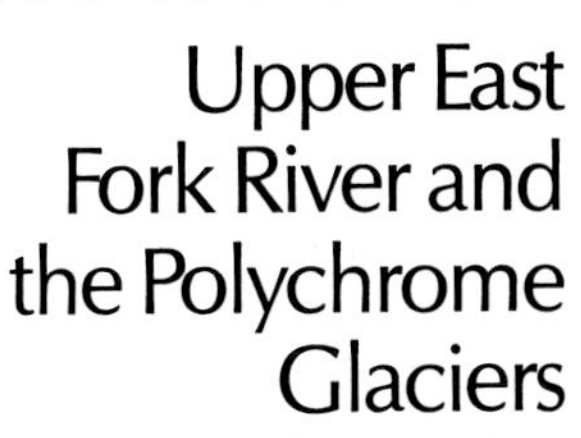

Upper East Fork River and the Polychrome Glaciers

Upstream from the East Fork River Bridge along the Park Road, the East Fork River branches into more than five streams. The first two branches, the largest ones, flow south from small glaciers through glacial valleys. The other branches of the East Fork River flow from narrow finger-glaciers called the Polychrome Glaciers. Halfway to their confluence, the streams enter an open tundra plain, locally called the Plains of Murie.

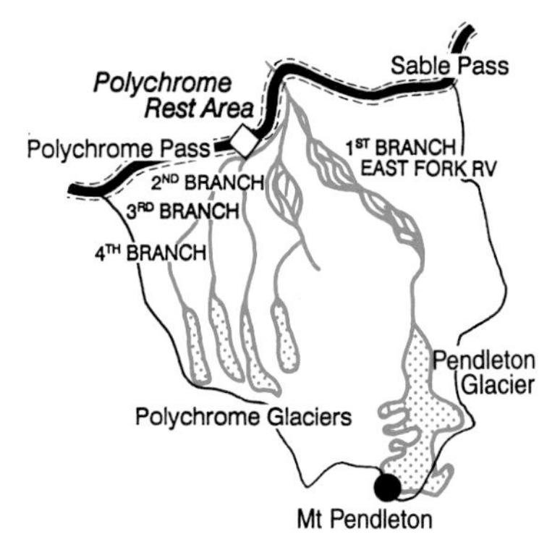

Flora and Terrain:

All the East Fork branches flow along gravel bars. Between the branches on the Plains of Murie the vegetation consists of dry and moist tundra with low and high willow groves scattered throughout. Although willows can get high, this is not true tree cover. The high hills that contain the Polychrome Glaciers and the glacier valleys of the first two branches consist of scree slopes and rock outcrops, poor rock for climbing or traveling. Some ridges are occasionally climbed, though the rock cover makes this dangerous.

Wildlife:

Caribou travel across the Plains of Murie throughout the summer, occasionally forming large groups. They may be found even in the glacial valleys of the first two branches. Grizzly bears can be expected anywhere in this area from the upper hills to the plains. Dall sheep inhabit the upper hills, along with marmot and pika. Moose wander and feed in the heavier willow growth.

Rivers and Streams:

Before the East Fork River branches out, it can be very difficult to find a braided section to cross. After that it is much easier.

2nd Branch East Fork River

Glaciers and Mountaineering:

As in most of the Alaska Range in the eastern part of the park, not much mountaineering is done here. The exception is Mount Pendleton, more than 7,000 feet (2,130 m) high. Although small compared to others in the park, it can be dangerous. Access to the standard climbing route is up the first branch glacier (also known as the Pendleton Glacier). Crevasses are a real hazard on this glacier, and the climb should be attempted only by experienced individuals. The Polychrome Glaciers are steep and covered with rock over much of their surface. Because of slope, loose rock, and crevasses, climbing can be dangerous.

Access from Park Road:
Mile 43 to Mile 50.

Topographic Maps:
Healy C-6, Healy B-6.

Upper Toklat River Valleys

The upper Toklat River valleys are two glacier-carved valleys that contain the East and West branches of the Toklat River. Both branches originate from glaciers nestled against the north slopes of the Alaska Range. The valleys are prominently "U-shaped," with a river bar that in places widens to more than a mile. The Toklat branches wander back and forth across the bars. The hills on either side of the river valleys rise to more than 7,000 feet (2,130 m) and are composed of a variety of rock types and colors. Many of the slopes are scree-covered and dangerous.

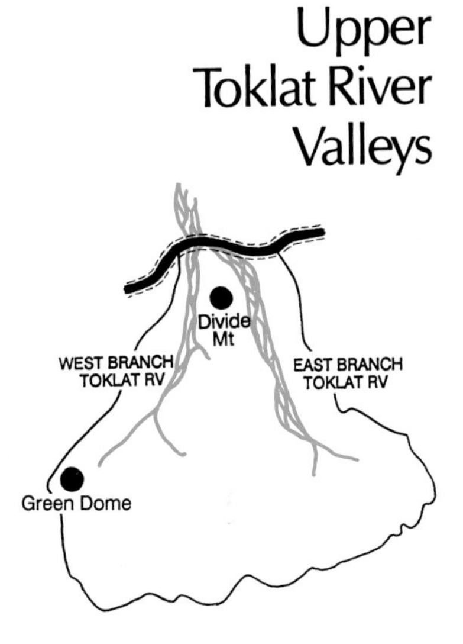

Flora and Terrain:

The wide river bar is bordered by low, dry tundra and sparse willows. On the lower elevations of the slopes dry tundra is the predominant ground cover. The middle and upper slopes of the high hills are a mixture of scree and jagged rock outcrops. There are no trees in the valleys. Visibility is mostly unobstructed along the river bars due to low vegetation and slope.

Wildlife:

Dall sheep abound in the high hills, particularly in early summer. Small groups of caribou travel the river bars at various times in the summer. Grizzly bears are usually found on the bars but can be seen at times in the upper hills. Valleys sustain high densities of soapberries, and bears can be seen feeding here in late summer. Marmots and pikas prefer habitat in the river headwaters and higher elevations.

Rivers and Streams:

Each valley contains a branch of the Toklat River. Crossing these rivers can vary from easy to extremely difficult. The rivers branch near the glaciers, making crossing easier, although it is harder to find braided segments near the headwaters. Traveling up either branch from the Park Road does not require a crossing.

East Branch of Toklat River

Glaciers and Mountaineering:

Rock type and physical geography preclude much mountaineering in this area. Five small glaciers feed the branches of the Toklat. Some are easily accessible, but all have crevasses and can be treacherous.

Access from Park Road:
Mile 50 to Mile 54.

Topographic Maps:
Healy B-6, Healy C-6, Mount McKinley B-1, Mount McKinley C-1.

ALASKA RANGE

Highway and Thorofare Passes

South of the Park Road between the Toklat and Thorofare river drainages, this area is made up of high and low hills with small creeks flowing south. Two passes, Highway and Thorofare, open south of the Park Road and divide the drainages. The hills are mostly scree slopes with patches of tundra, and some are climbable. The hills afford a view into the drainages to the east and west and into the higher mountains of the Alaska Range.

Flora and Terrain:

Small creeks flow over gravel bars and slopes support only dry tundra. There are few willows and no trees. The scree slopes should be considered dangerous, and the farther upriver, the steeper the grade.

Wildlife:

Caribou traverse the two passes parallel to the road. Grizzly bears are found in the low to middle elevations, and sometimes Dall sheep can be seen in the hills.

Rivers and Streams:

There are no hazardous waterbodies.

Glaciers and Mountaineering:

Although there are no large mountains, there are a few peaks in the 5,000- to 6,000-foot (1,524 to 1,829 m) range, such as Gravel Mountain, Green Dome, Stony Dome, and other unnamed hills. There are no glaciers in this area.

Access from Park Road:
Mile 54 to Mile 64.

Topographic Maps:
Mount McKinley B-1.

Mount McKinley from Stony Hill

Mount Eielson and Upper Thorofare River

The two streams that join north of Mount Eielson are the Thorofare River and Upper Glacier Creek. The Thorofare River flows south from Sunset Glacier at the base of Sunset Peak. Sunrise Creek, flowing from Sunrise Glacier, enters the Thorofare about 4 miles (7 km) downstream from the headwaters. The Thorofare River turns west and meanders across the milewide Thorofare Bar at the base of the Eielson Bluffs and Eielson Visitor Center.

After passing west of Mount Eielson, Upper Glacier Creek flows into the Thorofare River. In contrast to the wide glacial valley the Thorofare River travels along, Upper Glacier Creek flows through a narrow channel between hills on the east and the lateral moraine of the Muldrow Glacier on the west. Glacier Creek originates at the base of Anderson Pass, one of the few passes in this part of the Alaska Range. Halfway to the Thorofare Bar, Intermittent, Crystal, and Wolverine Creeks—all originating in the high hills to the east—converge at Upper Glacier Creek.

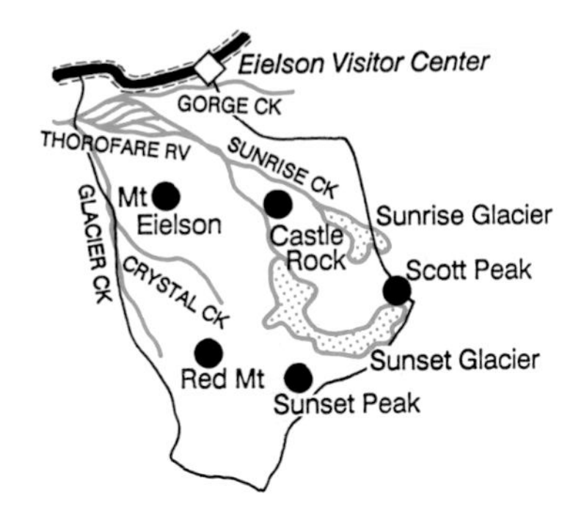

Flora and Terrain:

Vegetation in this area consists primarily of dry tundra with some small groves of willows. The Thorofare River flows across a wide bar from the headwaters to the confluence with Upper Glacier Creek. Upper Glacier Creek flows over river bars and into narrow canyons, but is still crossable. Most of the slopes are covered with loose scree and rocky outcrops resembling the hills in the upper Toklat and East Fork river systems. There are no trees.

Wildlife:

Grizzly bear range throughout this area, along with Dall sheep in the high elevations and caribou on the bars. Marmot and pikas inhabit the hills and lower regions of Anderson Pass.

Hiker along Thoroughfare River Drainage

Rivers and Streams:

The Thorofare River can be treacherous to cross, depending upon the location chosen. Upstream from the Thorofare Bar, the river usually flows swiftly in one or two channels, and the footing underwater is poor. The river along Thorofare Bar (downstream from the Eielson Visitor Center) is very braided, and crossing here makes the few extra miles worthwhile.

To hike from the Eielson Visitor Center to Sunset Glacier, you must cross the Thorofare River, because of a large cutbank, or climb more than 500 feet (152 m) to hike around it. Upper Glacier Creek may be running high but is usually not difficult to cross. Traveling upstream along this creek necessitates crossings, again due to cutbanks.

Glaciers and Mountaineering:

Many glaciers in this area can be safely climbed. The smallest is Sunrise Glacier, about 3 miles (5 km) up a canyon from the junction of Thorofare River and Sunrise Creek. Sunset Glacier, somewhat larger than Sunrise, is about 5 miles (8.5 km) from the Eielson Visitor Center, and it can be seen from there.

Muldrow Glacier is the largest north-flowing glacier in Alaska. In this unit, the glacier seems more gravel than ice, but under all the scree are all the same glacial hazards. Crossing the Muldrow to Pirate Creek can be very dangerous, especially near flowing water, which usually indicates an ice channel beneath.

Early and late season climbing can be dangerous, depending upon route. Most routes include some type of glacier travel, and have well-deserved reputations for terrible weather. Two challenging mountains to climb are Scott Peak (8,828 feet, 2,691 m) and Sunset Peak (7182 feet, 2189 m). Other mountains not as technical are Mount Eielson (5,802 feet, 1,768 m), Red Mountain (7,165 feet, 2,184 m), and Bald Mountain (5,285 feet, 1,611 m). Anderson Pass provides a route to the south side of the Alaska Range, crossing it at 5,400 feet (1,645 m).

Access from Park Road:

Mile 64 to Mile 68. Access also from Eielson Visitor Center.

Topographic Maps:

Mount McKinley B-1.

ALASKA RANGE

Upper McKinley Bar and Pirate Creek Drainage

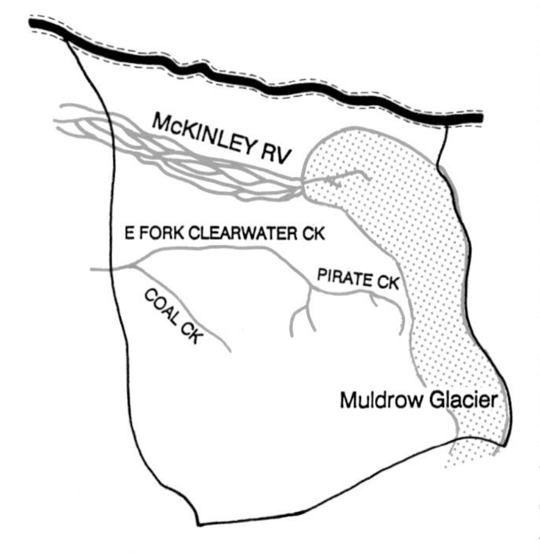

Pirate Creek area extends west from the Muldrow Glacier to Coal Creek and south from the Park Road to the high hills north of the Muldrow Glacier. Muldrow Glacier is in effect the south and east boundary of the region. The area between the Park Road and the McKinley River bar is gentle sloping tundra flats leading down to the river. The lower end of Thorofare River enters McKinley River on this broad bar. Upstream 6 miles (10 km) from the junction the Thorofare River flows through the Thorofare Gorge, a 4-mile long run where the river is a single channel. On the McKinley Bar, the river braids across the 1- to 2-mile (.6- to 1.5-km) -wide bar. Turtle Hill, a gentle tundra ridge approximately 1,000 feet (300 m) above the bar, divides the McKinley Bar and the East Fork of Clearwater Creek. Flowing into the Clearwater are numerous creeks originating in the hills to the south, among which are Coal and Pirate. The hills to the south reach a height of more than 7,000 feet (2,130 m) and are generally composed of a grey rock, much of it scree.

Flora and Terrain:

The vegetation here varies from mature spruce taiga forest along the McKinley Bar to dry tundra along the upper reaches of the hills to the south. Along the Thorofare and McKinley rivers, north of the bar, are small groves of poplar. Turtle Hill and the slopes south of the Park Road have a variety of tundra with willow groves and many tundra ponds. The Clearwater and other creeks south of Turtle Hill usually flow along river bars. The high hills have some scree slopes.

Wildlife:

Moose occasionally roam in the spruce forests along the McKinley River. Caribou wander throughout this area and are seen often on the McKinley Bar and Turtle Hill. Grizzlies are also common throughout this area, and black bear sometimes forage in the spruce forests. The tundra ponds on Turtle Hill and south of the road are home to beaver and muskrat and the resting place for migratory waterfowl.

Upper Glacier Creek

Rivers and Streams:

The McKinley River has been called the most difficult river to cross on the north side of the Alaska Range. Along the McKinley Bar the river can vary from two to 15 different channels and from ankle to above waist deep. The water flows from a nearby glacier at about 40°F or colder. At times it is uncrossable. Hikers should resist the urge to cross where there are only a few channels because the river will be deeper there.

The Clearwater usually poses no difficulty, but the Thorofare and some other creeks can be a different story. The Thorofare River is especially dangerous to negotiate because of its single channel, speed, and large boulders strewn about its channel. Your best bet is to cross above or below Thorofare Gorge.

Glaciers and Mountaineering:

The only substantial glacier in this area is the massive Muldrow. As described earlier, much of it is covered with scree and some vegetation. The section south of the high hills has more exposed ice and less scree, but access to it over the high hills is very dangerous. Some hills offer great vistas of the Alaska Range but there are no mountaineering peaks to climb.

Access from Park Road:

Mile 68 to Mile 82.

Topographic Maps:

Mount McKinley B-1, Mount McKinley B-2, Mount McKinley A-2.

McGonagall Pass

McGonagall Pass unit holds some historic significance. For many years it has been the way mountaineers climbing the Muldrow Glacier route of Mount McKinley accessed the mountain. Pack horses were used in the past to haul climbing gear for them. Now in the winter months, dog teams travel over McGonagall Pass to leave caches of gear for climbers following in the late spring. Although there is no maintained trail to the pass, there is a trail from the Wonder Lake vicinity to the McKinley Bar. This 2-1/2 mile (4-km) trail goes through a large spruce forest and ends at the bar. The rest of the way to the pass includes a traverse of Turtle Hill and its tundra ponds, a crossing of Clearwater Creek, and travel up the Cache Creek drainage to the pass. Two miles (3.5 km) below McGonagall Pass you'll find the fork to Oastler Pass on the east side of Oastler Mountain. From these passes are superb views of the upper Muldrow Glacier and Mount McKinley, Mount Brooks, and the other peaks of the Alaska Range.

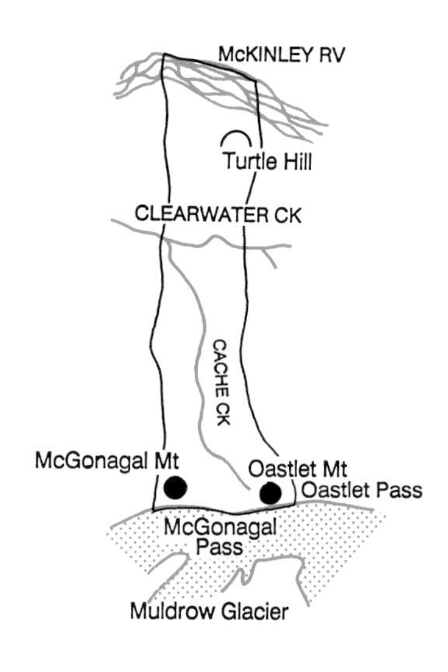

Flora and Terrain:

The vegetation and terrain is similar to the description in the Pirate Creek section. McGonagall Pass is approximately 5,700 feet (1,765 m), while Oastler Pass is 5,500 feet (1,512 m). The drop down to the Muldrow Glacier from these passes is short, approximately 100 feet (33 m), but very steep. Running along the northern margin of the Muldrow is a stream in a gully, which can be difficult and very dangerous to cross.

Wildlife:

Wildlife is similar to that of the Pirate Creek section.

Rivers and Streams:

As previously stated, crossing the McKinley River can be extremely hazardous. Plan on the crossing taking three or four hours. Be very careful of any moving water on the Muldrow Glacier.

Special Notes:

The McKinley Bar Trail starts 1/2 mile east of Wonder Lake Campground. Overnight camping along this trail, in its vicinity, or on the north half of the McKinley River is prohibited (day use status only here). To be camped out of view from the Park Road, parties must be off the river bar.

Many climbing parties try the Muldrow Glacier route each year. If you come across any gear at or near the pass, please leave it and inform a ranger upon your return. A climbing party may be depending on it!

Glaciers and Mountaineering:

The upper Muldrow Glacier probably appears more like what you expected a glacier to look like than did its lower end. There are a few scree lines and some crevasses. Crevasse danger is extreme at the Lower Ice-Fall. As for mountaineering, McGonagall Pass is an access to the peaks known as "Denali's Children," as well as Mount McKinley itself. For information on Mount Brooks, Mount Silverthrone, and the other "Children," turn to the mountaineering chapter later in this book.

Access from Park Road:

The McKinley Bar Trail is marked along the road approximately 1/2 mile (1 km) east of the campground. Access to the river bar doesn't necessarily have to be from the trail, which is mucky and wet in many spots due to permafrost melting. This trail illustrates why trails in Denali are discouraged.

Topographic Maps:

Mount McKinley A-2, Mount McKinley B-2.

ALASKA RANGE

Muddy River Drainage

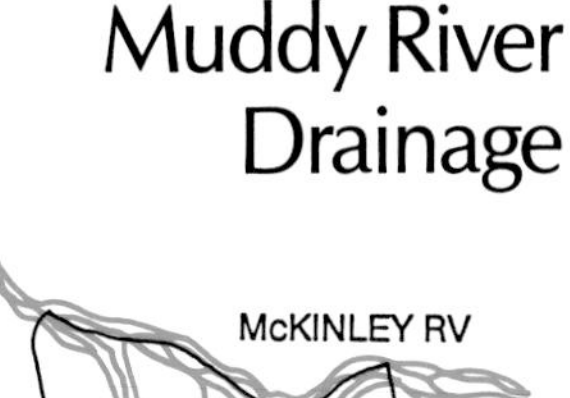

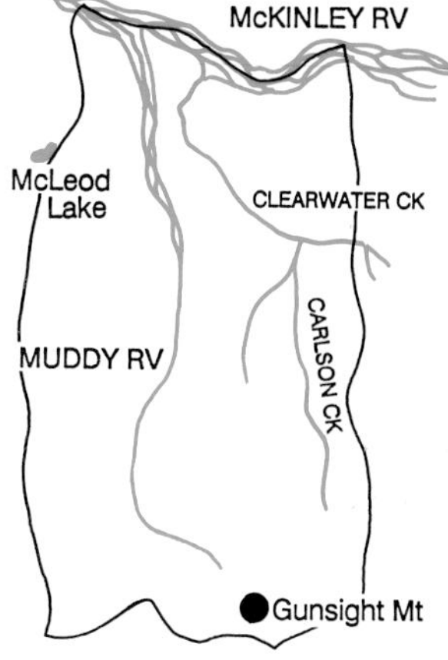

This area encompasses three tributaries of the McKinley River—the Muddy River, Clearwater Creek, and McLeod Creek. The eastern end of this unit includes the western end of the Turtle Hill ridge and Clearwater Creek where Carlson Creek enters it. The northern boundary is the McKinley River Bar, from approximately 4 miles (7 km) upstream from the confluence of the Clearwater to the beginning of Eagle Gorge. The western boundary is McLeod Creek and the southern boundary is the Alaska Range. This large area rises from an elevation of 1,600 feet (490 m) on the McKinley River to more than 6,000 feet (1,800 m) in the foothills of the Alaska Range. It is directly north of Mount McKinley and the Wickersham Wall and is, in fact, so close at some places in the southern section of this area Mount McKinley itself is not visible.

Vegetation and Terrain:

From the scree-covered slopes in the south to the spruce and alder along the McKinley River, vegetation varies markedly. Most of the ground between drainages is a mixture of wet and moist tundra with many tundra ponds, including McLeod Lake. Up close these tundra "flats" actually are an unending series of small hills and mounds. Though the upper section of Clearwater Creek is a gravel bar, the last few miles of the large waterway flow through a narrow canyon. The Muddy River flows across a large gravel bar, as does the McKinley before Eagle Gorge. The upper few miles of the Muddy is similar to parts of Thorofare Gorge.

Wildlife:

Caribou commonly graze throughout this area during the summer, along with grizzly bear. Moose may be found in the low, brushy elevations and near the McKinley River. The numerous tundra ponds are home for aquatic mammals and waterfowl.

Rivers and Streams:

The largest river here is the McKinley, discussed earlier. The Muddy River can at times be more difficult to cross than the McKinley because it doesn't braid as much, and it can be a major obstacle. The lower Clearwater is one channel and deep, but as its name suggests, you can see the bottom. You'll find the other creeks easy to cross except during flood.

Glaciers and Mountaineering:

Peters Glacier, a large glacier flowing past the Wickersham Wall from Peters Basin northwest of Mount McKinley, is the source of the Muddy River. The Peters Glacier has recently surged and extruded a vast jumble of broken ice on its surface. Travel along or across the glacier is impossible. A result of the recent surge is that the actual glacier terminus is many miles north of where it is shown on the topographic map. Though this area edges on the Alaska Range no high peaks occur. This area provides access to peaks near Mount McKinley and to Mount McKinley itself.

Hikers at the headwaters of Muddy River

Access from Park Road:

Since there is no direct access from the road, the best route is from Wonder Lake via other units.

Topographic Maps:

Mount McKinley B-2, Mount McKinley B-3, Mount McKinley A-2, Mount McKinley A-3.

ALASKA RANGE

The West End

The West End is the generic term given the western section of the Denali Wilderness west of the Muddy River. Few people travel to this area during the hiking season. Though it often appeals to true wilderness lovers, access is difficult. Lower elevations

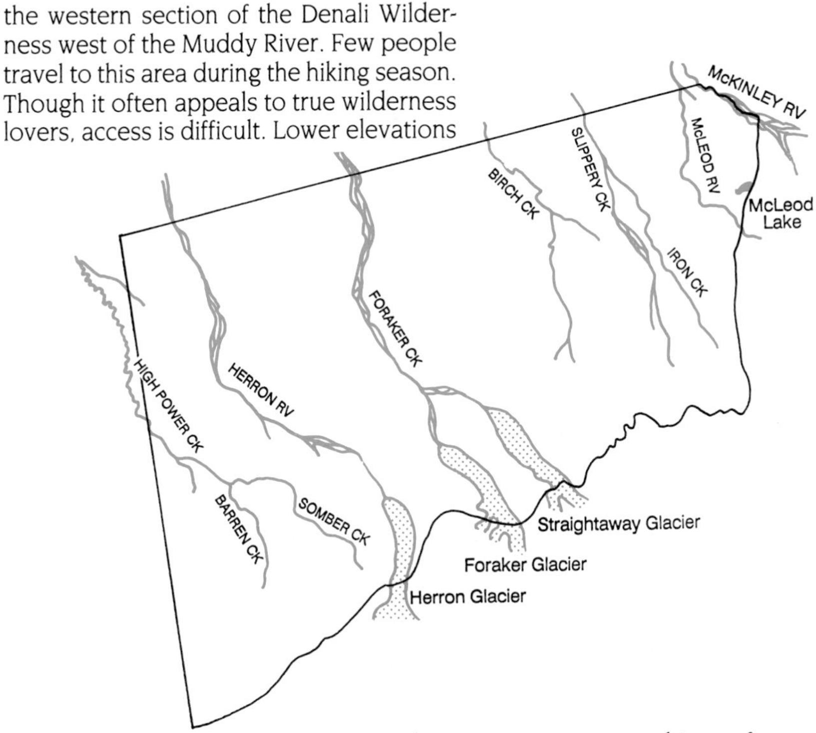

in the north (to 1,600 feet (520 m)) are dense taiga spruce stretching as far north as you can see. As you travel towards the Alaska Range and south, you will gradually enter the foothills of the range. Many large glaciers and their respective river systems flow north between notches in the foothills of the Alaska Range.

Vegetation and Terrain:

Taiga forests cover the flats, but above the 2,000 foot (620 m) level you will find open tundra, much of it dry, with some heavy brush. Dry tundra and exposed rock are the rule on the flanks of the foothills, which are mostly unvegetated scree slopes with exposed crumbly rock. Most of the waterways flow over gravel bars. At the snouts of glaciers you'll see moraines and, at some, miles of scree piles.

Glaciers and Mountaineering:

Many large and small glaciers extend over this region. Straightaway and Peters glaciers are good examples of broken-up glaciers, which make for slow going. The three largest glaciers in this unit are Herron, Foraker, and Straightaway. Smaller glaciers include Birch Creek and the glaciers of Peters Dome. You can access the high peaks of the Alaska Range via Peters Pass to Peters Basin on the Peters Glacier. Keep in mind, however, that the foothills north of the Alaska Range reach more than 10,000 feet (3,050 m), many are glaciated, and they are not casual climbs.

Access from Park Road:

There is no direct access from the Park Road. Most hikers go from Wonder Lake via the Muddy River unit. Average hikers take a minimum of three days to reach it from Wonder Lake. (That's five to six days just to reach the West End and return), and the hike includes crossing many rivers, such as the McKinley and Muddy.

Topographic Maps:

Mount McKinley A-3, B-3, A-4, B-4, A-5, B-5, Talkeetna D-4.

Wildlife:

Caribou are common, and grizzly bears are often spotted above treeline. Black bears inhabit the taiga. Rock mammals are found in the foothills.

Rivers and Streams:

The numerous streams and rivers here range from difficult crossings (McKinley) to some you can jump across. Generally, large glaciers spawn large rivers that may be challenges to cross. Also, because of the size of the glaciers daily fluctuation in river level can be substantial. Foraker and Herron rivers and Slippery, Birch, and Highpower creeks are all known to be difficult to traverse at times.

Straightaway Glacier and the Alaska Range

ALASKA RANGE
The South Side

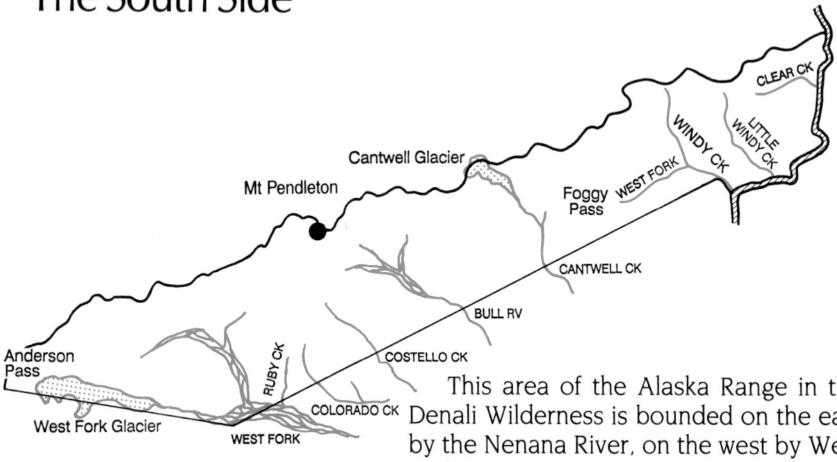

This area of the Alaska Range in the Denali Wilderness is bounded on the east by the Nenana River, on the west by West Fork Glacier, and on the north by the Alaska Range divide. A number of drainages flow from the Alaska Range south and east with high and low passes separating them. Windy Creek at the eastern end of this area flows from an east fork that begins at Windy Pass (to Riley Creek and Sanctuary River) and a west fork flowing from Foggy Pass. The west side of Foggy Pass provides access to upper Cantwell Creek. High passes west of Cantwell Creek afford access to upper Bull River. Easy Pass is between Bull River and a branch of the West Fork of the Chulitna River. By traveling either the West Fork Glacier or an unnamed glacier, Anderson Pass in the Alaska Range and Upper Glacier Creek north of the range can be reached. These passes and drainages are surrounded by steep hills, some reaching over 7,000 feet (2,260 m).

Vegetation and Terrain:

Most of the creeks and rivers in the upper valleys flow through glacial valleys and along river bars. Higher elevations are covered with dry tundra. Farther downstream willows, dwarf birch, and extensive groves of alders make some areas impassable. Spruce cling to the banks of Windy Creek, but trees are scarce in other parts of the area.

Wildlife:

Caribou, sheep, and grizzly bear inhabit the area. Moose feed only in areas of thick vegetation, such as Windy Creek.

Rivers and Streams:

Some of the large rivers in this area occasionally flood. You will find the West Fork of the Chulitna and the Bull River easiest to cross upstream. Cantwell Creek is large but usually less treacherous to cross. Some hikers follow the West Fork to reach the Parks Highway (Route 3) near Broad Pass, which entails crossing the tricky Middle Fork of the Chulitna.

Glaciers and Mountaineering:

Small and medium-sized glaciers feed all creek and river headwaters in the Alaska Range. Cantwell Glacier, which flows north to one branch of the Teklanika River, also flows south and forms Cantwell Creek. Near Easy Pass to the north are glaciers around Mount Pendleton. The West Fork Glacier is the largest, trailing a scree line that travels up it most of the way to Anderson Pass. An unnamed heavily crevassed glacier to the north of the West Fork meets up with it near Anderson Pass. Many small "feeder" glaciers flow into both. Mountaineering is not advised, some smaller peaks up to 6,000 feet (1,800 m) offer good climbs. Due to more precipitation the slopes of the hills on the south side of the range are steeper than on the north side.

Access from Park Road:

The Park Road provides no direct access. Use other units, or hike through the passes in the Alaska Range.

Access from Highway:

George Parks Highway provides access between Cantwell and Broad Pass.

Topographic Maps:

Healy B-4, B-5, A-5, B-6, A-6, Mount McKinley B-1.

THE OUTER RANGE

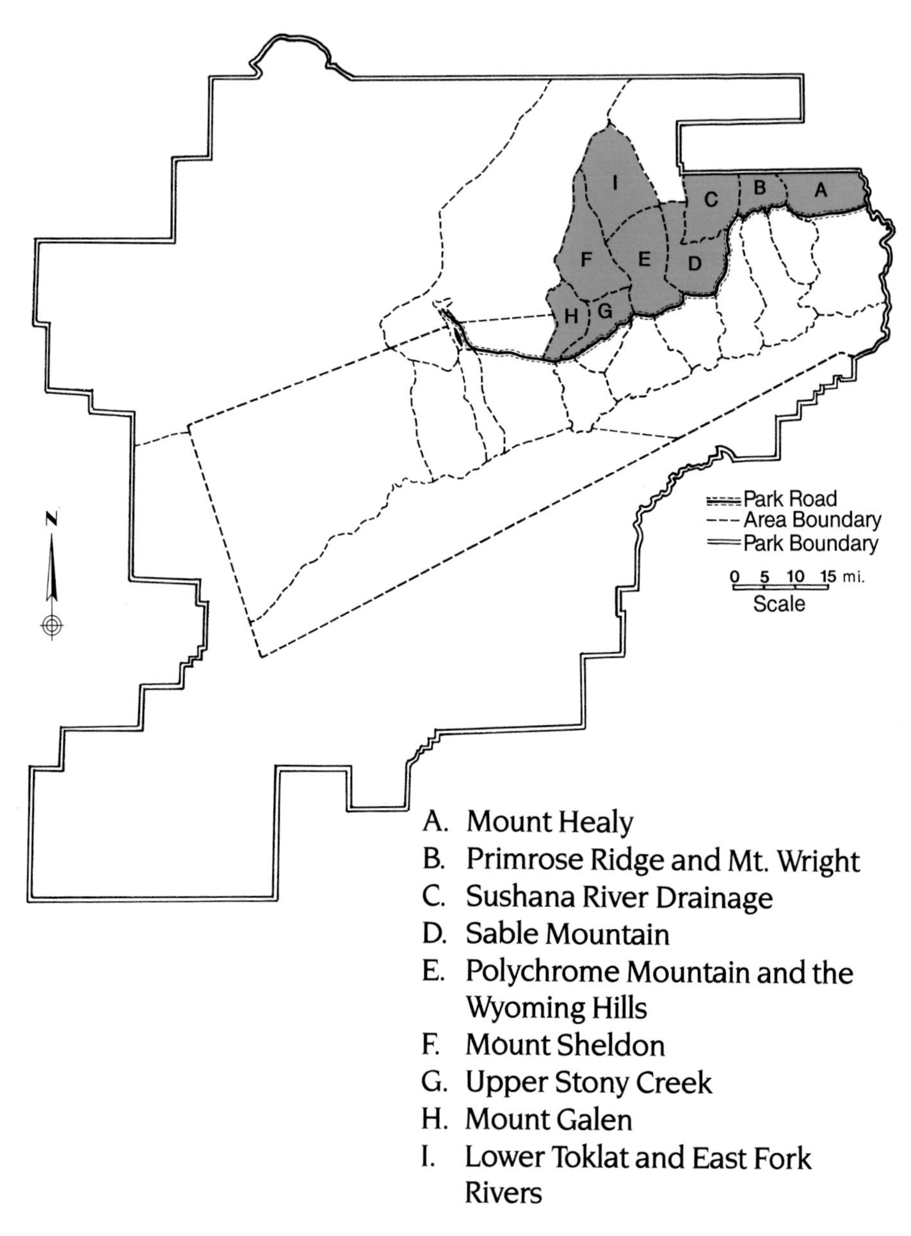

THE OUTER RANGE

Mount Healy

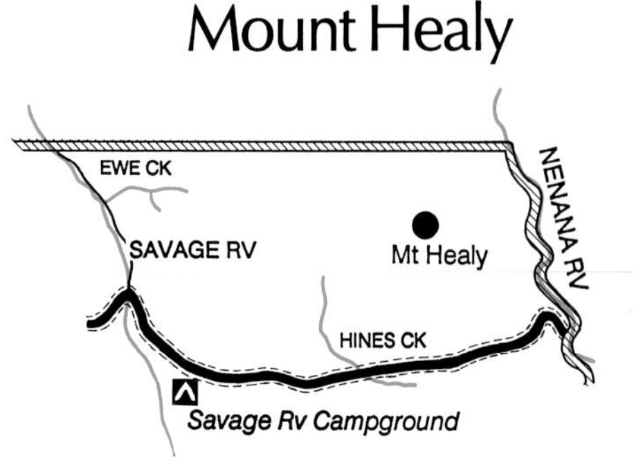

Mount Healy, also known as Healy Ridge, rises as a 10-mile-long ridge in the Outer Range from the Nenana River in the east to the Savage River canyon in the west. Its jagged peaks and spires in many places range as high as over 6,200 feet (1,890 m). Numerous small creeks flow south to the Jenny and Hines creek drainages and north to Ewe and Dry creek drainages. The Savage River flows north through the Outer Range in a canyon walled by Mount Healy to the east and Primrose Ridge (Mount Margaret) to the west. This 3-mile-long (5 km) canyon ends in a gravel bar.

Vegetation and Terrain:

The lower slopes of Mount Healy are covered with scree, dry tundra covers some of the slopes and saddles, and summits are exposed rock. As the slope flattens out at the base, the brush, mostly dwarf birch and willow, gets heavier. The only spruce occurs along the Savage River downstream from the canyon and along the eastern and southeastern flanks of the ridge, including the park headquarters and hotel area.

Wildlife:

Moose commonly roam the area's spruce forests and lower elevations with thick brush. Sheep range throughout the upper reaches of Mount Healy. Grizzly bear and some black bear are here, and caribou commonly migrate through the area early in the season near the Savage River.

Rivers and Streams:

The two major rivers here are the Savage and Nenana. The Savage River can be crossed almost anywhere except in the canyon, where uneven footing and fast flowing water make it too hazardous. The Nenana River is too deep and swift to ever be attempted. The other streams pose no danger.

Glaciers and Mountaineering:

There are no glaciers in this area. Climbing Mount Healy is possible, but beware of loose rock. Due to difficulty and exposure, a traverse of the entire ridge is rarely done.

Special Note:

There are two trails in this area—Healy Overlook and Savage Canyon. Healy Overlook Trail begins in the park hotel area and climbs halfway up the east end of Mount Healy. The Savage Canyon Trail begins at the Savage River Bridge along the Park Road and winds down the west side of the river. The latter is unmaintained, and is primitive. The southeastern section of this unit, the area around park headquarters and the hotel, is day-use only, and overnight camping is prohibited.

Access from Park Road:

Mile 0 to Mile 15.

Topographic Maps:

Healy C-5, Healy D-5.

Mount Healy from Park Road

Primrose Ridge and Mount Wright

Primrose Ridge, also known as Mount Margaret, is a 5-mile-long ridge between the Savage and Sanctuary rivers that runs east to west parallel to the Park Road. This flat-topped ridge, contrasting with neighboring peaked Mount Healy, reaches an elevation of 5,069 feet (1,545 m). Several small streams flow off the ridge to the north, forming Pinto Creek. The small streams to the south flow either into the Savage or Sanctuary river drainages. Mount Wright is a dome-shaped mountain between the Sanctuary and Teklanika rivers. These two rivers meet on the north side of Mount Wright, which rises to an elevation of 4,275 feet (1,303 m). The Teklanika and Sanctuary rivers flow through narrow gorges on either side of Mount Wright.

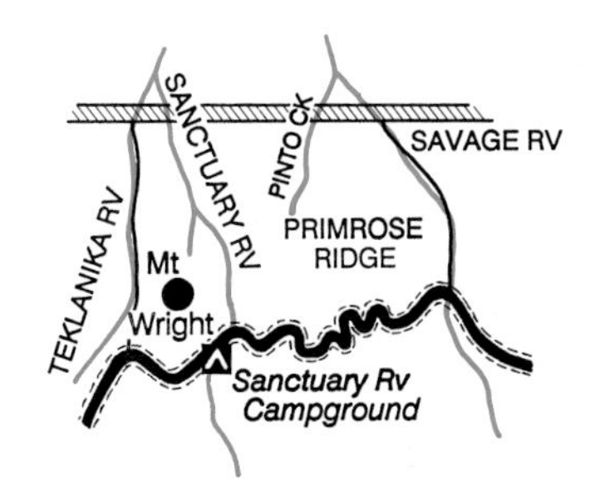

Vegetation and Terrain:

The tops of Primrose Ridge and Mount Wright generally are covered with dry tundra and with some rock outcrops. The slopes of these mountains are covered with dry tundra and patches of willows and dwarf birch, thickest in the lower parts of the drainages. Sparse spruce is found north and south of Mount Wright and scattered along the canyons. River canyons are narrow and steep and should be avoided.

Rivers and Streams:

The Teklanika and Sanctuary rivers are usually crossable on either end of their respective canyons, but should never be attempted in the canyons.

Glaciers and Mountaineering:

This area has no glaciers. Hikes up

Primrose Ridge and Mount Wright can hardly be called "mountaineering," but both afford beautiful views.

Access from Park Road:
Mile 15 to Mile 22.

Topographic Maps:
Healy C-5, C-6, D-5, D-6.

Primrose Ridge and Sanctuary River from Park Road

Sushana River Drainage

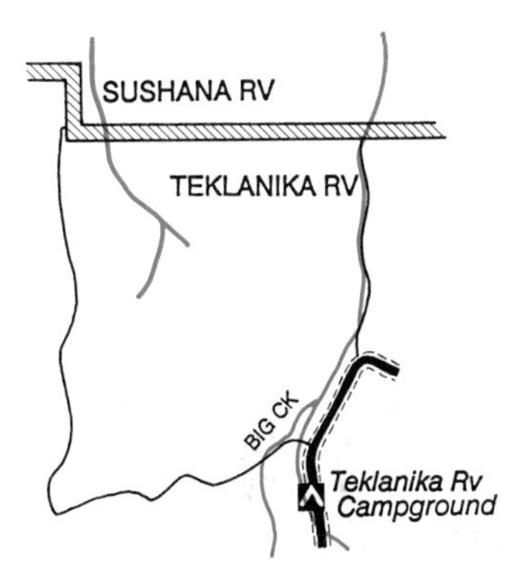

The Sushana River originates as six small streams flowing north out of a ridge of hills, locally called the Sushana Hills. This ridge, similar to Mount Healy but reaching only 4,510 feet (1,375 m), parallels the Teklanika River and comprises the west wall of the Teklanika River canyon near Mount Wright. The Sushana Hills are part of the Outer Range, and the Sushana River flows north out of the park. North of the Sushana Hills along the river are a series of low hills interspersed with low tundra.

Vegetation and Terrain:

Dry tundra and exposed rock are found high in the hills. Lower down is a mixture of moist and wet tundra. The Teklanika and Sushana rivers are lined with spruce and some willow and dwarf birch brush along the Sushana. Both rivers flow along river bars for most of their course.

Wildlife:

Sheep may be found in the highest elevations of the Sushana Hills, while below are moose and sometimes caribou. Grizzly bear range over the area also.

Rivers and Streams:

The largest river is the Teklanika River, and since it flows along a large bar, safe crossing areas can usually be found. The Sushana River is much smaller and a hazard only during high water conditions.

Glaciers and Mountaineering:

There are no glaciers in this area. The Sushana Hills are the only high point in this unit.

Sushana Hills and Teklanika River (Park Road on right)

Access from Park Road:
Mile 25 to Mile 31.

Topographic Maps:
Healy C-6, Healy D-6.

THE OUTER RANGE

Sable Mountain

The Sable Mountain area encompasses drainages and mountains in the Outer Range bordered on the east by the Teklanika River and Igloo Canyon and on the west by the East Fork River. Largest of the mountains in this area is Sable Mountain, 5,923 feet (1,805 m), towering over Sable Pass and the Park Road. Other peaks, such as Igloo Mountain, reach near and above the 5,000 feet (1,500 m) mark. Two drainages are found to the north of Sable Mountain—Tributary Creek flowing into the East Fork River and Big Creek flowing into the Teklanika. Many other streams drain east and west into these rivers. The East Fork River covers a wide gravel bar from the Park Road downstream approximately 8 miles (13 km) where it enters the narrow gorge of East Fork Canyon for about 7 miles (11 km). The hills of the Outer Range in this area are some of the most colorful and varied in composition in the park.

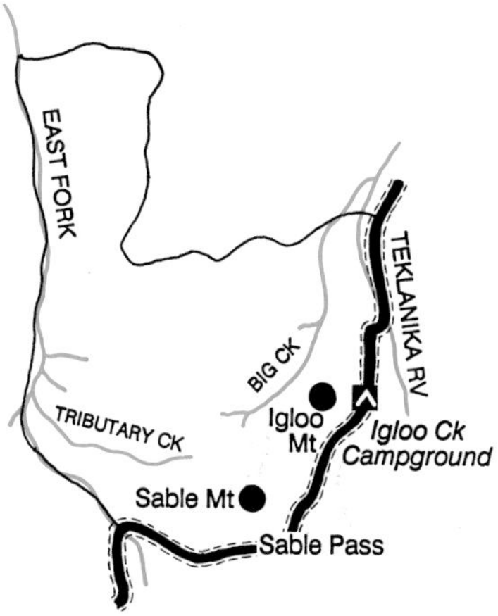

Vegetation and Terrain:

Dry tundra and exposed rock predominate high in the hills. Some of the hills, such as Igloo Mountain, are nearly bare of vegetation on their flanks. Thick willows and other brush grow along the small drainages. Small spruce groves dot the Teklanika, East Fork, and Big Creek. With the exception of some cutbanks, the East Fork River south of the canyon is fine for walking, but many river crossings are required.

Wildlife:

Dall sheep graze throughout the hills of the Outer Range, sometimes dipping down into Igloo Canyon. Grizzly bears are very common at all elevations, caribou may be seen on the river bars, and moose are often found near the Teklanika River and Big Creek.

Rivers and Streams:

The East Fork River is the largest river. On the wide river bar south of the canyon the river braids enough for easy crossings at low and medium water. The river narrows to one channel in the canyon and at times is impossible to cross. All the other streams pose no crossing problems due to high water, but there may be thick brush along their margins.

Glaciers and Mountaineering:

There are no glaciers. Many small mountains offer safe, nontechnical climbs, and you are sure to catch some spectacular views.

Special Note:

The southern boundary of this area (south of Sable Mountain) is the Sable Pass Wildlife Closure. Entry into this area is prohibited except by travel on the Park Road. This closure extends from south of Tattler Creek to east of the East Fork Bridge.

Access from Park Road:

Mile 31 to Mile 43. No access from the road in Sable Pass Closure.

Topographic Maps:

Healy C-6.

Big Creek and Igloo Mountain viewed from Sable Mountain

THE OUTER RANGE

Polychrome Mountain/ Wyoming Hills

The Wyoming Hills comprise the heart of the Outer Range. Here the range stretches approximately 13 miles north to south, in contrast to the single ridge of the Outer Range at Primrose Ridge and Mount Healy. There are numerous multicolored hills throughout this area, including Polychrome Mountain (5,790 feet, 1,756 m) and Cabin Peak (4,961 feet, 1,512 m). As in the Sable Mountain unit, there are many small streams throughout the hills, draining east into the East Fork River and west into the Toklat River. Some passes exist between the two rivers, such as Cabin Divide.

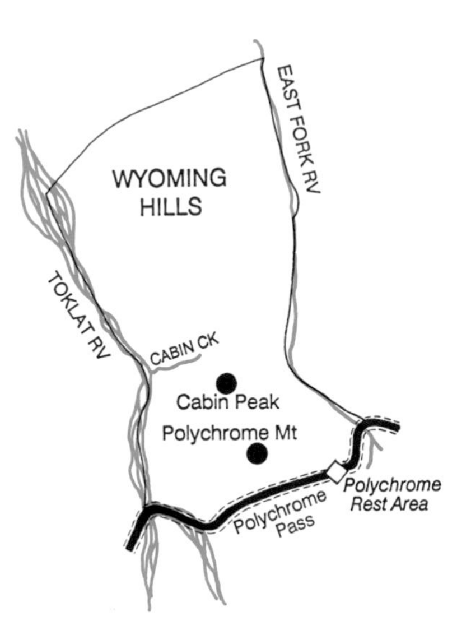

Vegetation and Terrain:

Vegetation and terrain are similar to that in the Sable Mountain area. Spruce grows along parts of the Toklat River. Scree and rock outcrops cover Polychrome Mountain.

Wildlife:

Dall sheep abound on the hills, and grizzly bears have a high concentration throughout the region. Caribou pass through the area all summer long. Marmot and other rock mammals inhabit the higher elevations.

Rivers and Streams:

The East Fork River has been described in the previous chapter. The Toklat River is larger than the East Fork but does not flow through a canyon and has a wide gravel bar offering many sites for crossing. In high-water, however, use extreme caution as conditions quickly can become treacherous.

Lower East Fork River Bar

Glaciers and Mountaineering:

There are no glaciers. The mountains and hills are similar to those found around Sable Mountain.

Access from Park Road:

Mile 43 to Mile 53.

Topographic Maps:

Healy C-6, Mount McKinley C-1.

THE OUTER RANGE

Mount Sheldon

Mount Sheldon, 5,670 feet (1,728 m), is located in the Outer Range between the Toklat River and lower Stony Creek. An impressive mountain, it overlooks the flats to the north of the range. To the west lower Stony Creek flows between Mount Sheldon and an unnamed ridge to the west. At the northern end of this unit Stony Creek enters the Clearwater Fork near the Stampede Mine area.

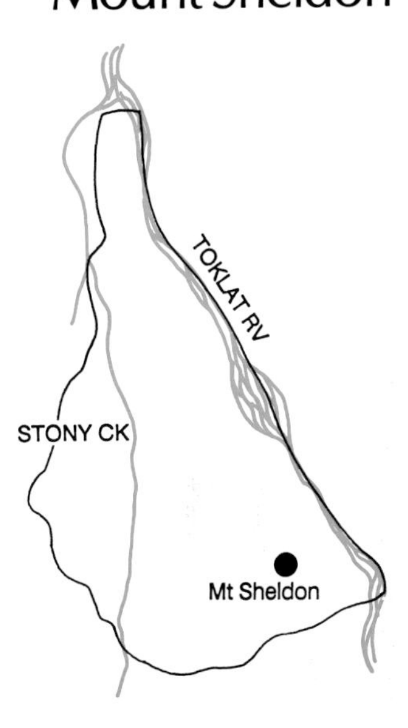

Vegetation and Terrain:

Exposed rock and dry tundra are found in the upper elevations. Spongy moist tundra covers the flats north of Mount Sheldon. Spruce and high willows grow along the gravel bar of the Toklat River. High willow predominates along Stony Creek.

Wildlife:

Sheep occasionally graze on Mount Sheldon, and moose, grizzly bear, and black bear forage in the lowlands. Caribou travel through the area.

Rivers and Streams:

Both the Toklat and Stony have gravel bars and braided channels, so crossings can be found. During high water the Toklat can be hazardous to uncrossable.

Glaciers and Mountaineering:

There are no glaciers. Mount Sheldon and other hills of the Outer Range are the high spots in this unit, affording excellent views of the vicinity.

Access from Park Road:

There is no direct access from the Park Road to this unit. Access is through other units.

Topographic Maps:

Mount McKinley C-1, Mount McKinley D-1.

THE OUTER RANGE

Upper Stony Creek

The area between the Toklat River on the east and Boundary Creek to the west, north of the Park Road and south of Mount Sheldon, is the Upper Stony Creek unit. Stony Hill, between Highway and Thorofare passes, is in the western third of this area. Stony Creek flows along the east side of the hill and Little Stony Creek on the west. The creeks meet north of Stony Hill, and Stony Creek meanders for approximately 6 miles until Boundary Creek enters it. These are the main drainages in this area, and between the 5,000 to 6,000-foot (1,500- to 1,800-m) hills of the Outer Range. Other small streams flow west and east. Stony and Little Stony creeks near Stony Hill (4,508 feet, 1,374 m) flow through small canyons, and after they meet the river widens into a gravel bar. Thorofare Ridge, towering over Eielson Visitor Center at 5,629 feet (1,716 m) has the Park Road to its south and the upper reaches of Moose Creek to the north.

Vegetation and Terrain:

Most of this area is above treeline. Spruce is only found along the Toklat River, and willow borders Stony Creek downstream from Stony Hill. Dry tundra prevails, and upper elevations have exposed rock and scree slopes. Some dwarf birch mixed in with dry tundra cling to the higher slopes.

Wildlife:

Dall sheep graze on Thorofare Ridge and the ridge west of the Toklat River. Caribou commonly use Thorofare and Highway passes as their migration route. Grizzly bears are quite common.

Rivers and Streams:

Except for the Toklat, there are no large rivers to cross. Stony Creek can be harder to cross downstream but usually poses no problem to hikers.

Glaciers and Mountaineering:

There are no glaciers. Some of the ridges afford a good climb, but scree and crumbly rock may pose a hazard.

Access from Park Road:

Mile 53 to Mile 68.

Topographic Maps:

. Mount McKinley B-1, Mount McKinley C-1.

Stony Creek canyon

THE OUTER RANGE

Mount Galen

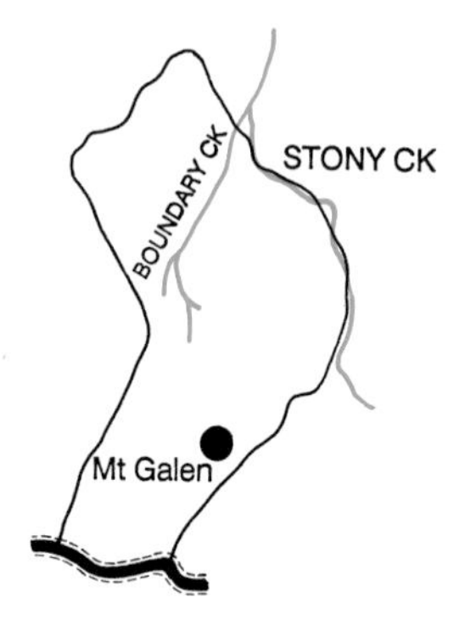

Mount Galen, a rounded, dome-shaped peak (5,022 feet, 1,531 m) northwest of Thorofare Ridge, is the last true peak of the Outer Range. West of Mount Galen the land is lower and more rolling in character up to the Kantishna Hills. Between Mount Galen and Thorofare Ridge flows the upper part of one branch of Moose Creek along a small gravel bar. A low pass exists between Moose Creek and an unnamed creek to the east that flows into Stony Creek.

Vegetation and Terrain:

Low to high brush, primarily willow, grows along Moose Creek. Low brush fades away to dry tundra as you go higher on Mount Galen. A combination of wet and moist tundra and occasional thickets of willow and tundra ponds cover the tundra flats and hills surrounding Mount Galen.

Wildlife:

Caribou travel along the creek and across the tundra, and moose and grizzly bear also range over the area.

Rivers and Streams:

Although a challenge downstream, Moose Creek here is no problem to cross and neither are the unit's other water bodies.

Glaciers and Mountaineering:

There are no glaciers, and Mount Galen is the only mountain. Although a simple climb, the southeast side is much steeper and is covered with loose rock.

Alaska Range from summit of Mount Galen

Access from Park Road:
Mile 68 to Mile 72.

Topographic Maps:
Mount McKinley B-1.

THE OUTER RANGE

Lower Toklat and East Fork Rivers

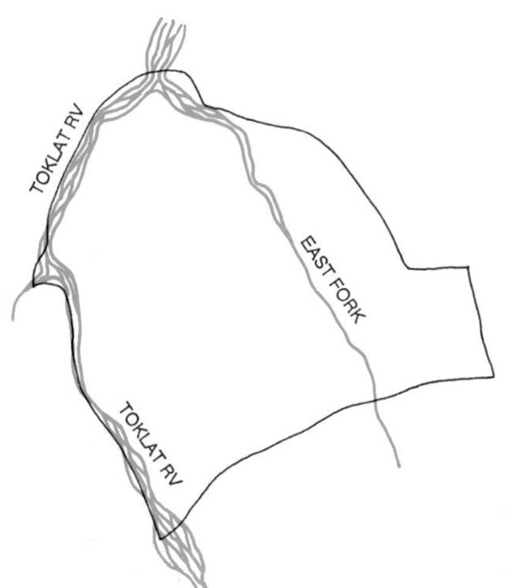

This somewhat remote area encompasses the Toklat and East Fork rivers north of the Outer Range and south of the Denali Wilderness boundary. The two rivers meander over large gravel bars heading north. Tundra plains slowly rise from the rivers south towards the hills. Throughout the flats small streams flow north into one or the other river.

Vegetation and Terrain:

Large spruce and some birch line the rivers. Most of the small stream banks support large, thick willows. On the flats the vegetation ranges from low tundra to dwarf birch and willow.

Wildlife:

Moose, caribou, and grizzly bear are throughout the area.

Rivers and Streams:

Although the rivers flow over gravel bars, the Toklat and East Fork rivers have significantly increased in water volume downstream from the Park Road, and crossings may be difficult. Crossings during high water may be impossible.

Glaciers and Mountaineering:

There are no glaciers or large mountains in this area.

Access from Park Road:

There is no direct access from the Park Road. Access is via other areas.

Topographic Maps:

Mount McKinley C-1, D-1, Healy C-6, D-6.

THE KANTISHNA HILLS

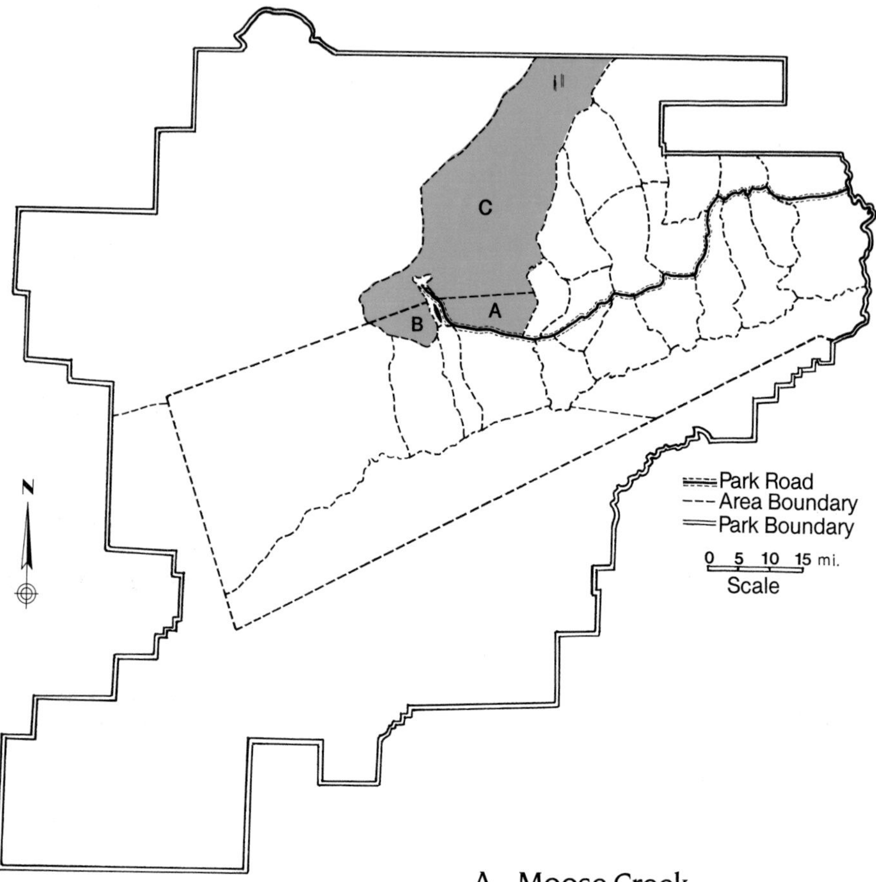

A. Moose Creek
B. McKinley Bar West
C. The Kantishna Hills

THE KANTISHNA HILLS

Moose Creek

Moose Creek flows west between low, tundra-covered hills. As it reaches the southern end of the Kantishna Hills, the main fork is joined by the North Fork of Moose Creek. A few miles beyond this junction, Jumbo Creek links up from the south. At this point Moose Creek enters the primary area of the Kantishna Mining District.

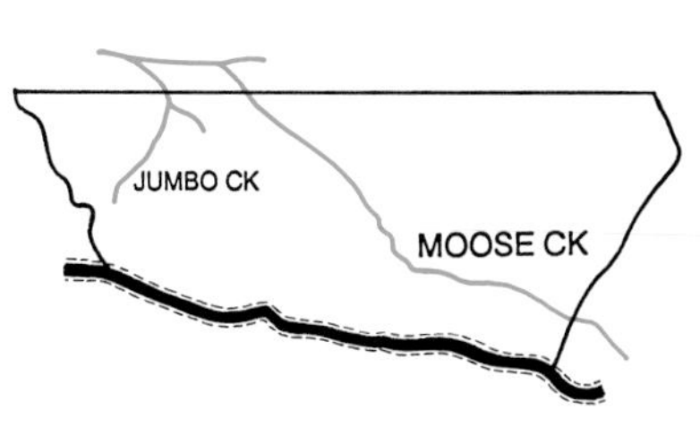

Vegetation and Terrain:

Except for a few areas along Moose Creek and the sides of a few hills, little tree cover is found. The variety of tundra types and heavy brush can make lower elevations difficult to travel cross-country. Higher elevations are less boggy and brushy. Much of Moose Creek is a gravel bar.

Wildlife:

Moose range throughout the lowlands, especially near Moose Creek. Caribou graze the area throughout the summer and grizzly and some black bear also forage here. The many tundra ponds support a wide variety of waterfowl and aquatic mammals.

Rivers and Streams:

Moose Creek is the only large water body, and as you travel downstream it becomes increasingly difficult to cross, especially after the two branches join.

Glaciers and Mountaineering:

There are no glaciers and no mountains in this area, only low tundra hills.

Special Note:

The lower section of Moose Creek enters the Kantishna Mining District. This is an active mining area, and some of the land is private property. Abandoned mining sites may still be privately owned. Please respect others' properties and stay away from mining claims.

Access from Park Road: Mile 72 to Mile 80.

Topographic Maps: Mount McKinley B-1, B-2, C-2.

THE KANTISHNA HILLS

McKinley Bar West

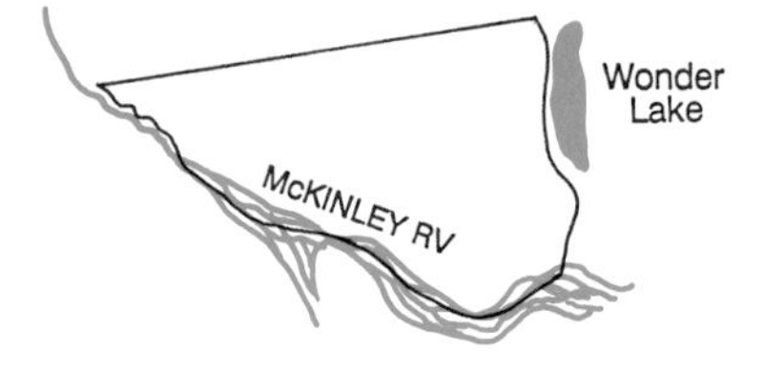

This area encompasses roughly a triangle, with Wonder Lake to the east, the west end of the Kantishna Hills to the north, and the McKinley River to the south. Here is a series of low tundra hills interspersed with small and medium-sized tundra ponds. From elevations of 2,500 to 3,000 feet (760 to 910 m) near the hills and Wonder Lake, the land gradually descends to less than 2,000 feet near the river. At the southeastern corner is an open grassy swamp.

Vegetation and Terrain:

Spruce trees and some poplar grow along the McKinley River and the swamp. All types of tundra cover the rest of the terrain, interspersed with willow and dwarf birch that become dense at times. Alder groves are found along the McKinley Bar across from the Muddy River. The McKinley River flows over a wide gravel bar. At drought or during dry times, the swamp provides for easy level travelling.

Wildlife:

The caribou, moose, grizzly and black bear are joined by other wildlife inhabiting tundra ponds. Many portions support aquatic mammals such as beaver, and birdlife is profuse.

Rivers and Streams:

At the western end the McKinley River leaves the bar and enters Eagle Gorge. Here the river is one channel, swiftly flowing between steep walls. Never attempt to cross the river here, and avoid travelling along its banks.

Glaciers and Mountaineering:

There are no glaciers or mountains in this unit.

Special Note:

The eastern boundary of this area is in the Wonder Lake day-use-only closure. Overnight stays are prohibited. If you can see Wonder Lake, you are still in the closure.

Access from Park Road:

Access is primarily from Wonder Lake and the road within a mile of the campground.

Topographic Maps:

Mount McKinley B-2, Mount McKinley B-3.

View from swamp south of Wonder Lake campground

THE KANTISHNA HILLS

The Kantishna Hills

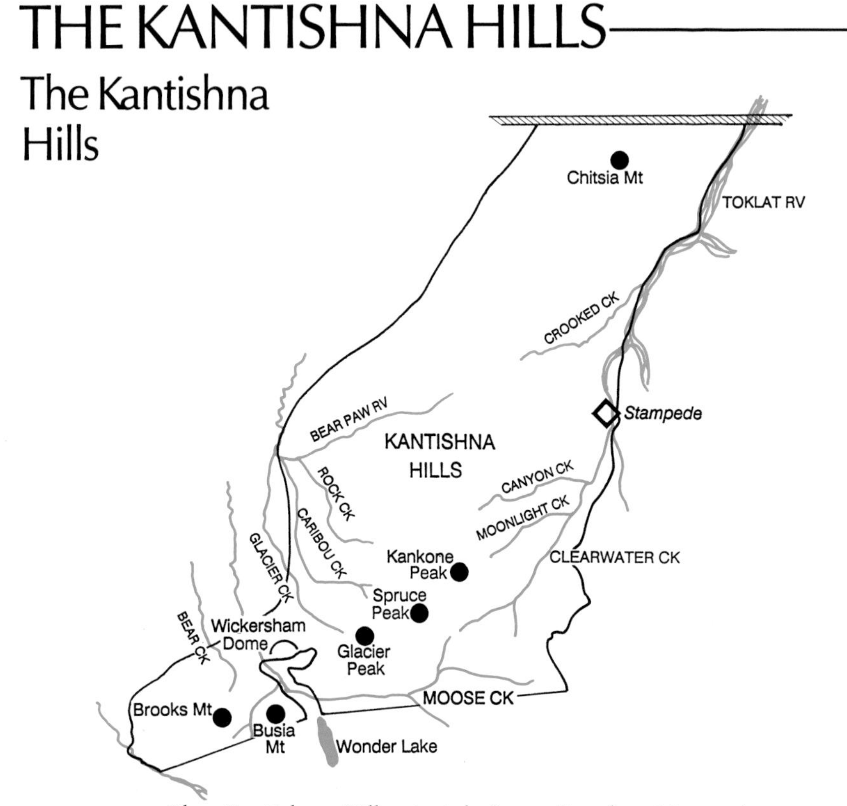

The Kantishna Hills stretch from Brooker Mountain west of Wonder Lake northeast to Chitsia Mountain near the junction of the East Fork and Toklat Rivers. This chain of low mountains is approximately 30 miles (50 km) long, and consists of a number of prominent peaks: Brooker Mountain (3,774 feet, 1,150 m), Busia Mountain (3,246 feet, 989 m), Glacier Peak (4,310 feet, 1,314 m), Spruce Peak (4,753 feet, 1,449 m), Kankone Peak (4,987 feet, 1,520 m), and Chitsia Mountain (3,862 feet, 1,178 m). Most of the summits are above treeline and are surrounded by taiga forests. Numerous small streams flow either east into the Toklat drainage or west into the Moose Creek and Bearpaw drainages. Lower Moose Creek passes through a small mining community called Kantishna. The abandoned Stampede mine site is located upstream from the junction of the Clearwater Fork and Toklat River. Most of this area in the New Park Additions is out of the Denali Wilderness.

Vegetation and Terrain:

Dry tundra covers the tops of the Kantishna Hills. Heavy brush is concentrated in the saddles between peaks. Thick brush and moist tundra predominate along the slopes and there are spruce with some birch at low elevations. Most stream banks are either thick with brush or piled over with mine tailings.

Wildlife:

Both grizzly and black bear inhabit the area as well as some caribou and moose. The heavy spruce is home to marten and other furbearers, but they are rarely seen.

Rivers and Streams:

The Clearwater Fork flows over a gravel bar, affording numerous safe crossing spots. Moose Creek, on the other hand, can be difficult to cross at high water. Most rivers and streams flow in narrow channels.

Glaciers and Mountaineering:

There are no glaciers. Many of the higher areas offer interesting climbs, but none would be considered technical.

Special Note:

As stated in the Moose Creek section, the Kantishna Mining District is an active mining area, much of it private property. Most of the side streams in the Kantishna Hills have been mined (placer mining). Abandoned and active trails and old, unimproved roads wind throughout the hills. The Stampede mine site is inactive, but it is still private property and poses many hazards to hikers. Stay away from all mining claims unless invited in by the owner.

Access from Park Road:

Limited shuttle-bus service extends beyond Wonder Lake to the beginning of the Kantishna Hills.

Topographic Maps:

Mount McKinley C-1, C-2, D-1, D-2.

NEW PARK ADDITIONS

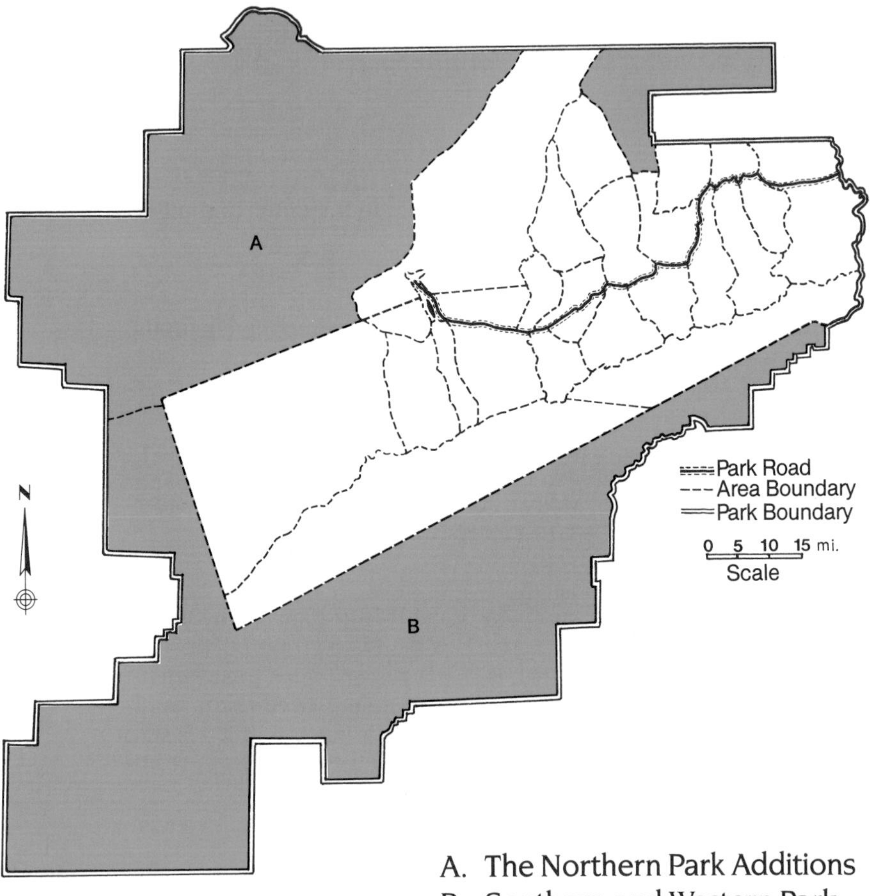

A. The Northern Park Additions
B. Southern and Western Park Additions

NEW PARK ADDITIONS

The Northern Park Additions

The Alaska National Interest Lands Conservation Act (1980) added land to the north, south, and west of the park. The northern and western additions increased and protected existing wildlife habitat, especially for highly mobile species such as caribou and wolf packs. The northern additions begin approximately 6 miles northwest of Healy. A section of land between them and the Denali Wilderness to the south, called the Wolf Townships, is owned by the State of Alaska and private individuals. Westward, beyond the lower Sushana River, the additions abut the Wilderness. From here on west the old trail to Stampede Mine is in the Additions. Much of this land is low hills and tundra flats.

Continuing westward, the Additions include the area where the East Fork River meets the Toklat River. This is in the vicinity of Chitsia Mountain, the northernmost of the Kantishna Hills.

West of the Kantishna Hills is a vast lowland taiga forest with elevations ranging from 500 to 1,670 feet (150 to 500 m). Throughout the lowlands slow-moving creeks and rivers meander back and forth, slowly feeding into the Kantishna River, which itself drains into the Tanana/Yukon river drainage. These waterways are Flume Creek, Bearpaw River, Bear Creek, Moose Creek, McKinley River, Slippery Creek, and many unnamed streams. Some areas of the taiga open into tundra swamps and ponds.

Birch Creek to the west is the boundary of additions classified as New Park Additions and Preserve. Management of Denali National Preserve to the west differs. The

Preserve/New Park Additions boundary is also north of the Kantishna River. This area north of the river contains low hills to 1,927 feet (587 m) and Chilchukabena Lake. Southwest of the hills is the junction of Birch Creek and the Muddy River (not the same river that flows from the Peters Glacier), and this merger forms the Kantishna River. The Muddy River is a slow-moving, meandering waterway that winds around a vast collection of lakes and swamps as it travels out of Lake Minchumina, a large lake just northwest of the park boundary.

Denali National Preserve west of Birch Creek is similar to the land between Birch Creek and the Kantishna Hills. Large rivers, such as the Foraker, Herron, and Highpower, meander past lakes and forests interspersed with low hills such as Castle Rocks.

Access to the northern New Park Additions and Preserve varies from hard to extremely difficult. The eastern New Park Additions can be entered by hiking, but it is impractical to consider hiking into areas such as Chilchukabena Lake. Winter access differs (see later section on winter park use) but is still difficult. Air access, though available, is costly, and the rewards usually do not outweigh the money and effort spent to get there.

Topographic Maps:

Two maps (1:250,000 scale) cover the entire northern New Park Additions and Preserve, Mount McKinley, and Healy. The large park map, also at 1:250,000 scale, covers this area, too. Quadrangle maps (scale 1:63,360), the type mentioned in previous descriptions, are available but to cover the entire area are too numerous to be practical for most hikers.

NEW PARK ADDITIONS

Southern and Western Park Additions

The Southern Additions to the park primarily were established to protect the entire mountain massif of Mount McKinley and that section of the Alaska Range. Much of this area will be covered under the "Mountaineering" section. The eastern end of the addition begins near the small community of Cantwell. The strip of land includes the lower ends of drainages such as Cantwell Creek, Bull River, and the West Fork of the Chulitna.

Farther west the New Park Additions include the lower reaches of the large glaciers flowing south from the Mount McKinley massif, such as the Ruth, Tokositna, Kahiltna, and Yetna. Most of this is above treeline, but thick vegetation covers lower areas.

A "bulge" on the western edge of the additions envelopes the Kichatna Mountains and much of the East and West Fork of the Yetna River. Three passes in the Alaska Range—Mystic, Shellabarger, and Simpson—lead to land west of the park boundary.

A small strip of land makes up the Western Park Additions. This adds land north of the Alaska Range near Heart Mountain and the Chedotlothna Glacier, the source of the Swift Fork of the Kuskokwim River. Travelling north, the land loses elevation, and the taiga begins. At the Cottonwood Hills (1,770 feet, 539 m), the New Park Additions become the Preserve.

Similar access problems are associated with the Southern and Western Additions as with the Northern Additions. In the south, another problem faces hikers. Alders are prevalent, and cross-country travel in the lowlands can be depressingly slow to impossible.

Topographic Maps:

The 1:250,000 park map covers this land, and it is also included on three other 1:250,000 maps: Healy, Mount McKinley, and Talkeetna.

MOUNTAINEERING

Denali National Park offers some of the most challenging mountaineering in Alaska. Mount McKinley (Denali), the highest mountain in North America, naturally receives the most attention, but climbers can find a number of challenges throughout the Alaska Range.

This section is not a mountaineering guide for the peaks of Denali National Park, but to acquaint you with the resources in the park. The community of Talkeetna is the center for mountaineering information. The rangers at Talkeetna Ranger Station specialize in mountaineering advice, and you should discuss your plans with them prior to any expedition except for the lower peaks. (Information on lower altitudes can be obtained at the backcountry desk when you get your backcountry permit.) To contact the Talkeetna Ranger Station, write to P.O. Box 588, Talkeetna, Alaska 99676 or phone: (907) 733-2231.

Peter's Dome Summit

The prime climbing season in the Alaska Range is short. Though a few hardy people have climbed Mount McKinley and other peaks in winter, most people make their attempts in May and June when temperatures are less extreme and snow conditions and storms less threatening.

From an attempt at McKinley's peak to a day trip up Scott Peak, all climbers should have the basic knowledge of glaciers, rope travel,

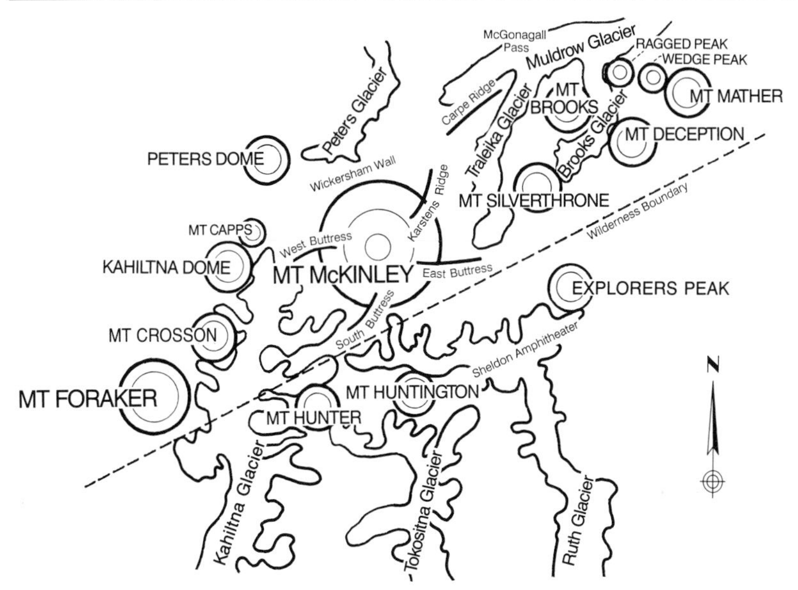

avalanches, and all general mountaineering skills. Do not underestimate the lower peaks or compare them with mountains of similar elevation in warmer climates. Continuous snow and ice cover begins near the 7,000-foot (2,100-m) mark. Lower peaks usually can be climbed in a single day from a nearby base camp. Mount Pendleton and Scott Peak, mentioned in previous chapters, are the two main peaks in this category.

In the immediate vicinity of Mount McKinley and Mount Foraker (Sultana) are a group of climbable peaks in the lower 10,000-foot (3,100 m) range sometimes referred to as "Denali's Children." East of McKinley a few of these peaks can be accessed by McGonagall Pass and the Muldrow Glacier. Across the Muldrow Glacier from McGonagall Pass are the intersections of the Brooks and Muldrow glaciers, and the Traleika and Muldrow glaciers. Between these glaciers are peaks such as Mount Brooks, Mount Deception, Ragged Peak, Wedge Peak, Mount Mather, Mount Silverthrone, Carpe Ridge, and the Tri-Pyramids.

West of McKinley the "Children" include Kahiltna Dome, Mount Crosson, Mount Capps, and Peters Dome. To the south of McKinley are Mount Hunter, Mount Huntington, and the peaks of the Sheldon (Ruth) Amphitheater. Most of these peaks are accessed from the Kahiltna Glacier or Ruth Glacier via bush plane from Talkeetna.

Mount McKinley and Mount Foraker are the two highest peaks in the park. While the difficult Foraker (17,400 feet, 5,304 m) is attempted by only a few groups each year, McKinley (20,320 feet, 6,194 m) attracts many parties each season. One reason for Mount McKinley's popularity is the variety of routes it offers. They range from basic (West Buttress), to difficult (Muldrow-Karstens Ridge), to highly technical (Cassin Ridge). The majority of climbers fly into the upper Kahiltna Glacier and climb the West Buttress. Although considered basic for a McKinley route, West Buttress still holds many challenges. Climbing parties may encounter problems with weather, altitude, and hypothermia.

East of Mount McKinley on the south side of the range is the Don Sheldon Amphitheater, previously known as the Ruth Amphitheater. This is an area along the Ruth Glacier where its many branches join. Surrounding the amphitheater and beyond it where the glacier enters the Great Gorge rise many peaks with sheer walls on the Ruth side. These peaks include Mount Dan Beard, Explorers Peak, Mount Barrille, Mount Dickey, and the Mooses Tooth. They range from 7,500 feet to over 10,000 feet (2,300 to 3,100 m) in elevation. These peaks provide high-quality rock faces for technical climbing. Access to the Amphitheater is by plane usually from Talkeetna.

Remember, mountaineering in Denali National Park is not simply facing the ordinary obstacles of most climbs. The severity of the Alaska environment adds to the difficulty. From weather extremes to remoteness, the Alaska Range provides added challenges to all who attempt to climb.

WINTER

Denali National Park is open year-round. The Park Road is not maintained in winter and is usually closed from the beginning of October to May, though this varies with conditions from year to year. With the Park Road and services beyond park headquarters closed, visitation drops dramatically. Access becomes a problem, as well, but for the intrepid winter camper, possibilities and rewards are limitless.

Mechanized travel, such as snowmachines, are illegal in the Denali Wilderness, but cross-country skiing, snowshoeing, and dog sledding offer exciting alternatives. The

Park Service does not maintain trails in the park, and conditions vary. Though skiers can often find a couple of feet of fresh snow on the south side of the range, bare tundra on the north side, which receives much less precipitation, can be encountered throughout the winter.

The river bars provide easy travel, though they are prone to high winds and may be snow free and ice covered. Metal-edged skis offer distinct advantages in such conditions as you will probably encounter bare tundra, rock, and ice along with scattered snow.

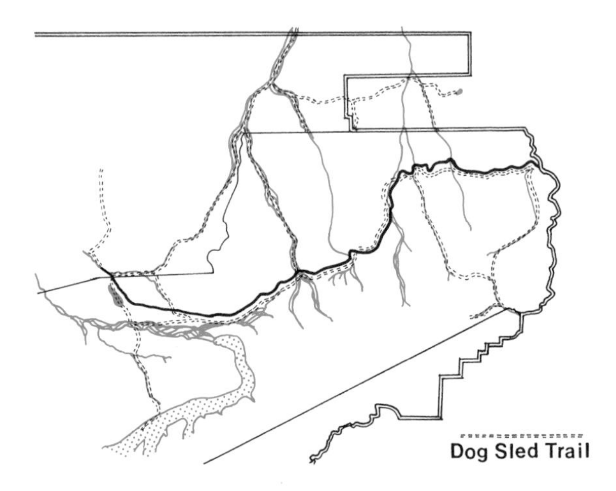

A handful of people travel in the park each winter by dogsled. Since the park maintains a sled dog kennel of approximately 25 to 30 dogs for winter patrols and other projects, good sled trails exist throughout the interior by springtime. (The park kennel provides no services to the public.)

A dogsled trip through the park can be the experience of a lifetime, even for a veteran musher. Trail conditions differ markedly from the well-maintained trails of Fairbanks and Anchorage. Before starting a trip, talk with the rangers at the park kennel about recent conditions and pick up a few tips.

Whether it be skis or dogpower, all parties going on an overnight trip into the park backcountry must stop at park headquarters to get a free permit and current conditions report. Even if you're not planning on overnighting, it's a good idea to check in at headquarters. The reduced daylight and intense cold of winter narrow your odds of success unless you plan well and prepare for all eventualities. Denali's winter environment is less forgiving than summer's. Self-sufficiency and caution should be uppermost in your mind.

—SPECIAL POPULATION ACCESS

Even the term Denali Wilderness brings to mind pictures of sweeping vistas of a stark tundra, steep, rock mountain slopes, and large glaciers. With no trails, bridges, or any man-made structure, it may seem daunting to all but the most fit. Even without the amenities that enable easy access in other parks, individuals of special populations can still enjoy wilderness aspects of the park. The National Park Service nationwide has made a commitment to making park experiences available to all Americans.

Though it is impossible for all people to travel everywhere in the backcountry, it is possible for everyone to experience some of what the park has to offer. A few of the established trails near the park entrance are accessible to people with limited mobility, including those in wheelchairs. The park runs one shuttle bus a day that is designed for wheelchair access. Once out in the park, you will find that even a short distance off the road you can get the "wilderness feeling."

Visitor center staff is eager to help all individuals of special populations enjoy the park. If you are interested in exploring the backcountry, no matter what your limitations, talk with the park rangers about how best to accomplish your goal.

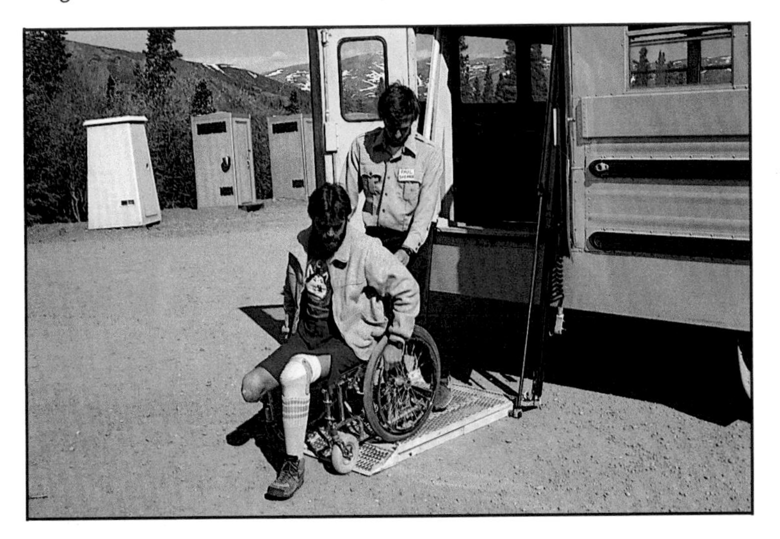

AFTERTHOUGHTS

The Denali backcountry offers a unique alternative to the more developed parks of the world. In this vast expanse of wilderness you can still test your skills and explore a land untouched by people. This freedom demands a heightened sense of responsibility for yourself and your group. You should know of and be prepared to deal with the hazards of the backcountry before you enter.

After reading this backcountry companion, you know something about how the park is managed, its resources, skill required, and possible hazards. You will help yourself and the park staff by consulting with them about the best trip plan for you. Even then, armed with this knowledge, you can never know of and prepare for every possible situation. Wilderness implies a bit of the unknown, and this aspect of Denali National Park is part of its appeal, part of its challenge.

Denali's uniqueness derives from the feelings it arouses in those who come to know it, different in each person. This, more than anything, is the true magic of the Denali Wilderness.

Photo Credits:

Page 1, 3 - William E. Ruth
4,6,7 - Jon Nierenberg
10 (top and bottom), 15 - N.P.S.
20, 30, 32, 38, 40, 42, 44, 47, 52, 55, 60, 62, 64, 66, 68, 71, 73 - Jon Nierenberg
75 - William E. Ruth
78, 86, 89 - Jon Nierenberg
91, 92 - N. P. S.
Front Cover - Robin Brandt
Back Cover - Jon Nierenberg